—

the

JEWISH FOOD HERO

COOKBOOK

50 Simple Plant-Based Recipes

for Your Holiday Meals

—

JEWISH FOOD HERO

Nourishing your mind, body, and spirit

Turner Publishing Company
Nashville, Tennessee
www.turnerpublishing.com

Cover design: One Plus One Design // Book design: One Plus One Design
Photography: Matkonation

Library of Congress Cataloging-in-Publication Data Upon Request

9781684422340 Paperback
9781684422357 Hardcover
9781684422364 eBook

Printed in the United States of America
18 19 20 10 9 8 7 6 5 4 3 2 1

——

TABLE OF CONTENTS

JEWISH FOOD HERO

Nourishing your mind, body, and spirit

INTRODUCTION

One week before Purim in 2012 there I was, living in rural Cambodia, the only Jewish person for miles, and desperately Googling to find a holiday menu that inspired me and was healthy for my family.

All the recipes I found made me feel like I was a Bubbe or Savta, and were not reflective of my or my daughter's generation. I wondered if poor health and weight gain was the "price to pay" for engagement in Jewish life.
I knew that I wanted to celebrate more Jewish holidays than I already was, but I wasn't confident I could do it on my own.

I dreamed about having a menu for every Jewish holiday that gave me the peace of mind and confidence for the healthy food I wanted to serve and the memories I wanted to create.

I never found the menu of my dreams—so I created my own instead.

The Jewish Food Hero Cookbook is my contributionto the Jewish community's efforts to increase healthy food on our tables.

My goal is that together we can create a new and healthy food future for the Jewish people, one that is connected to our most beautiful traditions while being grounded in the present.

Even though this is a cookbook, it's not just about the food and the final presentation. It's also about how you feel leading up to the holiday, and the ambiance you want to create from day one of your preparation. It's about your experience of the holiday itself and the memories you'll inspire for your family and your children for generations to come.

Cooking healthy holiday meals can be a form of creative expression, self-care, and love.

I see a different food future for the Jewish people. I'm so glad you're here and part of this vision.

To your health and inspiration,

Kenden

—

HOW TO USE THIS COOKBOOK

This cookbook contains menus for the ten major Jewish holidays.

Inspiration for the Menus
Each holiday section begins with the background on my inspiration for the menu. I've shared a range of personal stories and memories that are meaningful to me, and will, I hope, be meaningful for you, too.

Energetic Themes
Then I share an energetic theme for you. Use this energetic theme however it feels good to you—thinking about what the theme means to you as you shop and prepare the food, writing in your journal about the topic, or using it as a conversation starter at your table. There's no wrong way to do this.

Recipes and Ingredients
Each holiday menu includes one appetizer, a maindish, two side dishes, and a dessert. There is alwaysone recipe that can be prepared by children with adult supervision, indicated with an asterisk, and gluten-free options.

All the recipes in this cookbook use completely plant-based food (no animal products) and everyday kosher parve ingredients.

In a separate PDF that came with your cookbook purchase, you'll find shopping lists for each of the holidays and dishes.

It's the pairing of both traditional and modern, healthy food that will create the most satisfying, special celebration. For this reason, the recipes were created from our traditional and symbolic dishes for each particular holiday.

There are a few different ways you can use these menus:

- Cook the entire menu, from appetizer to dessert

- Pick a few dishes or ingredients to combine with your traditional holiday recipes

- Use one recipe from the menu to add to your holiday table Ready? Let's get cooking.

—

ROSH HASHANAH

—

www.jewishfoodhero.com

ROSH HASHANAH

The Inspiration Behind This Menu

In 2013, Rosh Hashanah was an impromptu celebration—the group of people joining us for the meal came together effortlessly and naturally. There were four adults, myself and my husband included, and five children under seven years old.

This led to the realization that we're celebrating and cooking for our children as much as we are cooking for ourselves. Children also have a role to play in the celebration, cooking, and meal; they must also findjoy at the table.

The father at that original Rosh Hashanah dinner was Moroccan, so I started playing with ingredients and recipes that had a Moroccan influence. I also began developing meals that would please children and adults, and tested them on my friends who joined me for Shabbat dinners.

This menu is simple with a Moroccan influence grounded in the sweetness (and reality) of celebrating holidays with children.

MENU

—

APPETIZER

Sweet Squash Spread
With Apple Slices

MAIN DISH

Ras El Hanout Vegetables
Over Couscous

SIDE

Citrus Carrot Salad

SIDE DISH

Garbanzo Beans in Red Sauce

DESSERT

*Spiced Stuffed Apples**

This recipe can be prepared by children with adult supervision.

—

SWEET SQUASH SPREAD WITH APPLE SLICES

—

—

SWEET SQUASH SPREAD WITH APPLE SLICES

Serves 8

This spread is just as lovely on challah, as it is served alongside fresh apple slices.

Tools

Large saucepan
Large bowl
Colander
Potato masher (or strong fork)
2 medium serving bowls
Small serving plate
Medium serving plate

Ingredients

4 cups butternut squash, peeled and diced
(from 1 medium butternut squash)
1 1/3 cups peeled and chunked Gala or
McIntosh apples
1 tablespoon lemon juice
1/2 teaspoon cumin
1 teaspoon cinnamon
Salt, to taste
Pepper, to taste
3 cups sliced apples
(from about 3 medium apples) to serve with
the spread

Optional:
Challah bread, sliced, to serve with the spread

Garnish:
Chopped green onion and cilantro

Instructions

In a large sauce pan:
- Place the prepped squash and apples, and cover with water until the water is 1 inch above the ingredients
- Boil until the ingredients are very soft

Over a large bowl:
- Drain with the colander and reserve the cooking liquid

Make the spread and season:
- Mash the cooked squash and apple together with a strong fork or potato masher
- Add the lemon juice, cumin, cinnamon, and salt and pepper to taste
- Add some of the reserved liquid, if needed

To garnish:
- Sprinkle with chopped green onion and cilantro

To serve:
- Separate the squash spread into two bowls
- Arrange the sliced apples on a small serving plate aside one of the bowls
- If using, arrange challah slices on a medium serving plate next to the second bowl

—

jewishfoodhero.com

Main Dish

RAS EL HANOUT VEGETABLES OVER COUSCOUS

—

—

RAS EL HANOUT VEGETABLES OVER COUSCOUS

Serves 8

This is a beautiful meal for friends and family that consists of a delicious
bed of couscous topped with roasted vegetables. The dish uses a traditional
North African spice blend and a little orange juice to add a fresh taste.

Tools

Large bowl
Small bowl
Orange juicer (manual or electric)
Blender
Rectangular baking dish (13 inch)
Aluminum foil
Steamer basket
Large serving bowl

Ingredients

*In this recipe, the vegetables can be prepared
with or without the peel.*
3 1/2 cups cubed zucchini
(from about 3 medium zucchini)
2 cups cubed turnips
(from about 2medium turnips)
2 1/2 cups sliced carrots
(from about 4 large carrots)
10 cups cubed eggplant
(from about 2 medium eggplants)
1 cup diced onion (from about 1 large onion)
1 cup seeded and diced red bell peppers
(from about 2 peppers)

Instructions

• Preheat the oven to 350 F

Prepare the eggplant:

• Place the eggplant cubes in a large bowl, cover with
  water, and add 1 teaspoon of salt

• Let soak for 20 minutes

• Drain and rinse when ready to roast

Make the spice blend:

• Combine all spices for the Ras El Hanout spice blend
  and set aside

• Squeeze 1 cup fresh orange juice

• Place 1 1/2 cups vegetable broth and the orange juice in
  a blender

• Add the desired amount of spice mixture (less if you
  like not too much spice and more if you like spicy food)
  and blend the ingredients

• Set aside

Roast the vegetables:

• Place all prepped vegetables (except for the bell pepper)
  evenly in a baking dish

• Pour the liquid spice blend over the vegetables

• Use your hands to evenly coat the vegetables

• Cover with aluminum foil

• Bake for 30 minutes, stirring occasionally

—

RAS EL HANOUT VEGETABLES OVER COUSCOUS

Serves 8

(...continued)

Ingredients

Ras El Hanout Spice Blend:
1/4 teaspoon ground cloves
1 teaspoon allspice*
1/2 teaspoon ground cumin
1 teaspoon ground ginger
1/2 teaspoon turmeric
1/4 teaspoon black pepper
2 teaspoons cardamom
1 teaspoon cinnamon
1 teaspoon coriander
1/2 teaspoon nutmeg

Optional:
1/4 teaspoon cayenne pepper

1 teaspoon salt, or to taste
1 cup fresh orange juice
1 1/2 cups vegetable broth

*If you cannot find allspice, you can make it yourself by combining equal parts cinnamon, cloves, and nutmeg.

Instructions

Prepare the bell peppers and finish roasting the vegetables:
- While the vegetables roast, steam the red bell peppers in a steamer basket over a medium pot with 1 inch of boiling water, for 5 to 10 minutes, then add to the baking dish in the oven, and roast for another 30 minutes, or until all the vegetables are soft

- Add more vegetable broth if needed during baking, to keep the vegetables moist

- Turn off the oven but do not remove the vegetables, so they stay warm

To serve:
- Mix the roasted vegetables with the steamed red bell peppers, and serve alongside the couscous in a large serving bowl

—

RAS EL HANOUT VEGETABLES OVER COUSCOUS

Serves 8

Couscous

Tools

Large saucepan with lid
Fork
Large serving platter
Small serving bowl for garnish

Ingredients

5 cups vegetable broth (or water)
4 cups instant couscous

Garnish:
Fresh mint

Instructions

- Boil the vegetable broth or water in a large saucepan

- Turn the heat off and stir in the couscous quickly

- Cover the saucepan and wait 10 minutes while the couscous cooks

- Taste the couscous after 10 minutes; if the consistency is still crunchy, add a little boiled water, then cover again to let the couscous absorb the water

- Use a fork to fluff the couscous

- Keep covered in the saucepan until you are ready to serve

To serve:
- Place couscous on large serving platter and cover with fresh mint (and other herbs if desired)

- Place the roasted vegetables in a separate serving bowl

- Place the fresh mint garnish in a separate small bowl and place on the table in case your guests would like to add more

- Serve hot

——

jewishfoodhero.com

CITRUS CARROT SALAD

—

—

CITRUS CARROT SALAD

Serves 8

This lightly sweet and spiced salad is served on a bed of fresh greens.
It's a refreshing accompaniment to the holiday menu.

Tools

Small skillet
Food processor with coarse grater attachment
or hand grater
Large salad bowl
Small bowl
Whisk

Ingredients

Salad:
1/2 lemon, sliced into thin rounds and
quartered
3 1/4 cups coarsely grated carrots
(from about 10 medium-sized carrots)
1 cup chopped dried apricots
1/4 cup minced parsley
2 teaspoons ground cumin
2 teaspoons ground cinnamon

Optional:
Sliced shallots or green onion to taste

Citrus Dressing:
1 teaspoon fresh orange zest
3/4 cup fresh orange juice
2 tablespoons lemon juice
Sea salt to taste
Pepper to taste

Instructions

Cook the lemon slices:
• Place the quartered lemon slices in a small skillet and sauté for 5 minutes

Prepare and season the rest of the salad:
• Grate the carrots using the food processor grater function (or a hand grater)

• In a large bowl, combine the carrots, dried apricots, and parsley

• Add the sautéed lemon slices, along with all of the remaining ingredients, and mix well

• Add shallots or green onion if using

Prepare the dressing:
• Combine all the ingredients in a small bowl and whisk to blend

To serve:
• Just before serving, pour the dressing over the salad and toss to coat

—

GARBANZO BEANS IN RED SAUCE

—

—

GARBANZO BEANS IN RED SAUCE

Serves 8

This dish is the perfect accompaniment to the couscous.
Children love, love, love this dish.

Tools

Large pot, if using fresh beans
Colander
Blender or food processor, if using fresh
tomatoes
Large saucepan
Medium serving bowl

Ingredients

3 cups cooked garbanzo beans
(from two 15-ounce cans of beans)
12 cups peeled and chopped tomatoes
(from about 12 medium tomatoes) or 4 cups
fat-free organic tomato sauce
3 cloves garlic
1 onion
1/4 cup vegetable broth or water
2 tablespoons tomato paste
1 tablespoon lemon juice

Spices:
1 teaspoon cumin
1/2 teaspoon cinnamon
1/2 teaspoon salt
1/4 teaspoon pepper

Garnish:
Chopped cilantro and green onion

Instructions

Prep the garbanzo beans:
• If you're planning to use dried garbanzo beans:
Soak the beans for 6 to 8 hours, or overnight, in a
large pot, then drain, rinse, and cover them with
fresh water by 1 inch

Cook and season the garbanzo beans:
If you are using canned beans: Rinse the beans in a
colander a few times and set aside, then skip ahead to
the next step.

• Bring the garbanzo beans to a boil, then reduce to a
simmer while covered on low heat

• Simmer for 2 hours or until soft. Add water as needed
while cooking and season with salt to taste at the end
(do not add salt at the beginning, or the beans will not
soften properly).

—

GARBANZO BEANS IN RED SAUCE

Serves 8

(...continued)

Instructions

Prep the tomatoes, and make the tomato sauce:

- If using fresh tomatoes, place the prepped tomatoes in a blender or food processor, and blend until smooth

- If using canned sauce, open the can and set aside

- Chop the garlic and onion

- Boil 1/4 cup of water in a large saucepan

- Add the onion and garlic to the saucepan and stir for 5 minutes

- Add the tomato sauce and tomato paste to the garlic and onion

- Stir in the cumin, cinnamon, lemon juice, salt, and pepper

- Boil for 30 minutes on low heat, stirring occasionally

Assemble the dish:

- Once the sauce is done, stir in the cooked beans, and cover until serving

- Transfer to a medium serving bowl

To garnish and serve:

- Sprinkle with chopped cilantro and green onion and serve family style at the table

---

Dessert

SPICED STUFFED APPLES

—

—

SPICED STUFFED APPLES

Serves 8

A revision of a grandmother favorite, these steamed apples are stuffed with nut butter, spices, and currants. They're delicious, simple, and sugar-free. These can be served cold or warm. If you want them warm, make sure to keep them in the oven until dessert time.

Tools

Apple corer
Small bowl
Large skillet with lid
Serving dish

Ingredients

8 medium Gala apples (or any baking apple)
2 1/2 tablespoons peanut or almond butter
2 1/2 tablespoons maple syrup
1/4 cup currants
2 teaspoons ground cardamom
1 teaspoon ground cloves
2 teaspoons ground cinnamon plus more for garnish
1/2 cup apple juice

Optional:
Non-dairy vanilla ice cream

Instructions

Prep the apples:

- Using an apple corer, completely core each apple

- Then, remove 1/4 inch from the bottom of each core. Set this piece aside.

- Make 6 vertical cuts around the top of the apple

- Reinsert the 1/4-inch core piece to fit into the bottom of each apple to act as a plug

Mix the filling:

- In a small bowl, use a fork to mix together the nut butter and maple syrup

- Stir the currants into the mixture

- Add the cardamom, cloves, and cinnamon to the mixture

Assemble the apples:

- Stuff each apple with a spoonful of the filling mixture

- Arrange the apples in a large skillet (make in two batches if needed)

- Pour the apple juice over the apples so it fills the bottom of the skillet

- Cover and steam, on medium heat for approximately 35 minutes, or until the apples are soft (add a bit of water during the cooking process if the liquid runs too low)

- Serve hot or cold, and add a scoop of non-dairy vanilla ice cream, if desired

—

—

YOM KIPPUR

—

www.jewishfoodhero.com

—

YOM KIPPUR

The Inspiration Behind This Menu

Many of us have had the experience of feeling as if we have to gorge ourselves in pre-fast and post-fast meals for Yom Kippur.

I wanted to create a menu that would encourage you to eat nourishing food and leave the table satisfied, but not overstuffed. This menu includes a nourishing and simple pre-fast meal, and a three-course post-fast meal. I paid particular attention to provide plenty of protein and nourishing carbohydrates at both meals.

The pre-fast menu is designed to be satisfying and sustain your body during the fast. The post-fast menu is meant to be soft, hydrating, and comforting.

(The Cardamom Coffee Cake can be eaten first, with tea, to really comfort you after the fast.)

Both menus were created to *ease* the body into and out of the fast.

It's worth nothing that the most important element is actually not on this menu—water. Hydration is very important, so be sure to place plenty of water at your table for both of these meals.

I've fallen in love with pasta and risotto in my adult years, and since rice and pasta are wonderful starches to give the body before and after the fast, Italian food seemed the perfect inspiration for this Yom Kippur meal.

—

PRE-FAST MENU

—

MAIN DISH

Creamy Lemon Pasta

SIDE

Pesto White Bean Salad

POST-FAST MENU

FIRST

Cardamom Coffee Cake*

SIDE

White Bean Vegetable Soup

MAIN DISH

Butternut Risotto

*This recipe can be prepared by children with adult supervision.

—

jewishfoodhero.com

Main Dish

CREAMY LEMON PASTA

—

—

CREAMY LEMON PASTA

Serves 8

This is a healthier (and vegan) re-make of avgolemono, or egg-lemon sauce.
In Sephardic Jewish cuisine, it's called agristada or salsa blanco.

Tools

Blender or food processor
Medium saucepan
Whisk
Large pot
Colander
Large serving bowl

Ingredients

3 cups vegetable broth
3 tablespoons lemon juice
3/4 cup silken tofu, drained
1/2 teaspoon turmeric
1 tablespoon plus 1 teaspoon sea salt, or salt to taste
1 tablespoon plus 1 teaspoon unbleached flour (or use gluten-free all-purpose flour)
1 1/2 pounds whole-wheat linguini, or gluten-free pasta of your choice

Garnish:
Fresh minced parsley

Instructions

Make the sauce:

- Place the vegetable broth, lemon juice, tofu, turmeric, sea salt, and flour in a blender and blend until smooth

- Transfer this mixture to a medium saucepan and heat gently, whisking periodically

- Cook for about 10 minutes, or until smooth and slightly thickened

Make the pasta:

- Bring a large pot of salted water to boil

- Add the pasta to the boiling water and stir well to prevent sticking

- Cook the pasta according to the package directions, stirring occasionally as it cooks

- Drain the pasta in a colander, then transfer to a large serving bowl

Assemble the pasta and sauce:

- Pour the sauce over the pasta, and toss to combine

- Serve lukewarm, topped with a sprinkling of minced parsley

—

jewishfoodhero.com

PESTO WHITE BEAN SALAD

—

—

PESTO WHITE BEAN SALAD

Serves 8

This salad is satisfying and fresh tasting. The beans provide some extra protein before the fast. It should be made 24 hours in advance to allow the beans to fully marinate in the dressing.

Tools

Small glass bowl
Colander
Large serving bowl
Blender or food processor

Ingredients

Salad:
1/2 cup thinly sliced red onion
(from 1/2 onion)
1/2 cup red wine vinegar
3 cups fava beans or cannellini beans
(from two 15-ounce cans)
1 cup thinly sliced celery
(from about 2 celery stalks)
1 cup coarsely shredded carrots
(from 3 medium carrots)
1/2 cup quartered artichoke hearts,
packed in water
8 fresh sage leaves, minced

Optional:
1/2 cup quartered pitted black olives

Pesto Dressing:
1 cup fresh basil
1 tablespoon pine nuts
1 tablespoon mustard
1 clove sliced garlic
1 tablespoon honey
1 tablespoon fresh lemon juice
Sea salt to taste

Instructions

Quick pickle the onion:
- Place the red onion in a small glass bowl with the red wine vinegar and mix well. Set aside for 10 minutes.

Assemble the rest of the salad:
- Drain the beans in a colander and rinse well under cold water

- Place the rinsed beans in a large bowl for mixing

- Add the prepped celery, carrots, drained artichoke hearts, sage leaves, the red onion and vinegar mixture, and black olives, if using

- Pour the pesto dressing (below) over the salad, and mix to coat

- Let marinate for up to 24 hours

Make the dressing:
- Place all the ingredients in a blender or food processor and blend until smooth

- Taste and adjust seasoning to taste

To serve:
- Garnish with quartered black olives if desired, and serve family style on the table

—

jewishfoodhero.com

28

First

CARDAMOM COFFEE CAKE

—

—

CARDAMOM COFFEE CAKE

Makes 12 individual Bundt cakes

Break the fast with a comforting cup of herbal tea and a sweet and warming coffee cake. The cake includes black currants and cardamom.

Tools

Large mixing bowl
Whisk
High-powered blender or food processor
Small bowl
Cooking oil
1–2 mini Bundt pans
Small mesh strainer for the powdered sugar

Ingredients

Dry ingredients:
1 cup unbleached, all-purpose flour
(can use gluten-free all-purpose flour)
1 cup whole-wheat pastry flour
(can use gluten-free all-purpose flour)
1 teaspoon baking soda
1 teaspoon baking powder
1 cup sugar
1/4 teaspoon sea salt
1/2 teaspoon ground cardamom
3/4 cup black currants

Wet ingredients:
1 teaspoon coconut oil
1 cup silken tofu
1 cup applesauce
2 tablespoons avocado oil
1–2 teaspoons fresh lemon juice
1 teaspoon all-natural vanilla extract
1/2 teaspoon almond extract

Sugar-nut filling:
1/2 cup chopped pecans
1/2 cup sugar, or alternative sugar blend
1 1/2 teaspoons cinnamon
1/2 teaspoon cardamom

Garnish:
Powdered sugar

Instructions

- Preheat the oven to 350 F

Prepare the dry mixture:
- Place all the dry ingredients in a large mixing bowl and whisk to blend

Prepare the wet mixture:
- Place all the wet ingredients in a blender or food processor and blend until smooth

Combine the two mixtures:
- Pour the wet into the dry ingredients and stir well, but do not overmix

Make the sugar-nut filling:
- In a small bowl, combine all the ingredients for the filling and stir to combine

Prep the Bundt pan and bake the cakes:
- Lightly oil the mini Bundt pan cavities

- Place a small amount of the sugar-nut filling on the bottom of each cavity

- Add a little bit of the batter on top of the filling

- Add the remaining sugar-nut filling

- Top with the remaining batter

- Bake for 45 minutes, or just until the center of the cakes spring back to the touch

- Cool completely before carefully inverting

To serve:
- Using a small mesh strainer, lightly sprinkle with sifted powdered sugar if desired

———

jewishfoodhero.com

Side

WHITE BEAN VEGETABLE SOUP

—

—

jewishfoodhero.com

WHITE BEAN VEGETABLE SOUP

Serves 8

This soup is light yet nourishing—a perfect dish for your meal to break the fast.
Garnishing each soup bowl with toasted bread pieces gives it just the right touch.
This soup can be made 24 hours in advance and warmed up after the fast.

Tools

Large soup pot
Individual soup bowls for serving

Ingredients

8 1/2 cups low-sodium vegetable broth
2 cups diced onion
2 cloves minced garlic
2 cups diced carrots (from 3 medium carrots)
1 cup diced celery (from 2 celery stalks)
1 cup diced tomatoes
(from 2 medium tomatoes)
3 cups cooked cannellini beans
(from two 15-ounce cans)
1 bunch kale, de-stemmed and ripped into
bite-size pieces
Sea salt and black pepper to taste

Garnish:
4 pieces of whole-grain bread, toasted and cut
into cubes
Fresh minced parsley

Instructions

In a large soup pot:

- Heat 1/4 cup of the vegetable broth over medium heat for several minutes

- Add the onion and garlic. Cook and stir for 10 minutes, adding small amounts of additional broth as needed to prevent sticking.

- Add the carrots, celery, and tomatoes. Cook and stir for another 10 minutes, adding a little more broth if needed.

- Add the cannellini beans and remaining broth. Cover and bring to a boil.

- Reduce the heat and simmer on low for at least 30 minutes, and up to 1 hour

- Add the kale, sea salt, and pepper, and simmer for another 10 minutes, or until the kale is tender. If you are making this soup 24 hours in advance, add the kale only when you are reheating it.

To serve:

- Ladle the soup into individual soup bowls, and garnish with bread cubes and a sprinkling of fresh parsley.

Main Dish

BUTTERNUT RISOTTO

—

BUTTERNUT RISOTTO

Serves 8

Risotto is a popular Italian classic, and this recipe is sure to please after the fast.
This recipe includes butternut squash, vegetables, and a slight sweetness from the white wine.
This dish can be made quickly following the fast.

Tools

2 small bowls for garnishes

Medium saucepan

Large saucepan

Soup ladle

Wooden spoon

Medium pot and steamer basket

Medium bowl

Large serving bowl

Individual bowls for serving

Ingredients

12 cups low-sodium vegetable broth

2 tablespoons water

2 cups diced onion (from 2 medium onions)

2 cups peeled and diced butternut squash

4 cups raw Arborio rice (do not rinse)

2 cups white cooking wine

Garnish:

1–3 dried apricots, thinly sliced

1 cup pomegranate seeds

Sugar snap peas

Instructions

Prepare the fruit garnish:
- Slice the apricots and prepare the pomegranate seeds. Place in individual bowls and set aside.

Heat the vegetable stock:
- Place the vegetable broth in a medium saucepan and warm over medium heat

Sauté the vegetables and deglaze the pan:
- In a large saucepan, heat the 2 tablespoons of water and add the onion. Cook and stir for 10 minutes, or until the onion is transparent.

- Add the squash. Cook and stir for another 5 minutes.

- Add the rice. Cook and stir for 5 minutes.

- Add the white wine. Stir constantly until the wine has been absorbed.

Cook the risotto:
- Using a soup ladle, add 1 cup of the hot vegetable broth and stir with a wooden spoon until it has been absorbed, stirring constantly

- Repeat with the remaining broth, adding 1 cup at a time, until all of the broth has been absorbed and the rice is tender with a creamy consistency

- This should take about 30 minutes total

- Feel free to add a little more broth if you like your risotto extra creamy

- When the risotto is finished, keep it covered until serving

———

jewishfoodhero.com

BUTTERNUT RISOTTO

Serves 8

(...continued)

Instructions

Prepare the sugar snap peas garnish:

- Steam the sugar snap peas until they are bright green,
  and then immediately remove from heat, place in a
  medium bowl, and set aside

To serve:

- Serve the risotto warm, garnished with the
  steamed sugar snap peas, pomegranate seeds,
  and thinly sliced dried apricots, in a large serving
  bowl or in individual bowls

—

SUKKOT

—

www.jewishfoodhero.com

—

SUKKOT

The Inspiration Behind This Menu

Since starting Jewish Food Hero, I've made a habit of researching Jewish food traditions in various locations around the world. I feel full of curiosity about the Jewish culinary journey through time and geographic space.

In May 2014, the *Forward* published an article called "Jewish Cuisine Makes a Stunning Comeback In Hungary." My favorite sentence from the article is this: "The lacy tablecloths and vintage light fixtures have all the retro-coziness of dinner at grandma's house."

I wanted to be there and experience this cozy feeling created by historical memory and good food. After all, my grandmother also used to make stuffed cabbage and create ambiance by using special tablecloths on her table.

The article inspired me to join in on this narrative, and create a healthy plant-based menu inspired by Hungarian food.

There's also one dish on this menu with a different influence. While I was planning the Hungarian menu in my head, I was flying back home to Asia from the U.S., and was watching a documentary about food in Korea. They had a spectacular idea for a salad using apple chips (which my daughter had just fallen in love with during our stay in the U.S.). And so, to complete this menu, I created a salad based on the Korean one from the show, and added a Hungarian twist to it.

—

MENU

—

APPETIZER
Mushroom Soup With Tofu Cream

MAIN DISH
Stuffed Cabbage

SIDE
Pickled Beets

SIDE
Apple-Cucumber Salad

DESSERT
Flodni Parfait*

*This recipe can be prepared by children with adult supervision.

—

jewishfoodhero.com

Appetizer

MUSHROOM SOUP WITH TOFU CREAM

—

—

MUSHROOM SOUP WITH TOFU CREAM

Serves 8

This lighter version of the classic Hungarian soup is a perfect way to begin your holiday meal.
This recipe makes enough for a cup of soup, enough for an appetizer as opposed to a meal.

Tools

Large soup pot
Blender or food processor
Decorative soup bowls for serving

Ingredients

5 1/2 cups low-sodium vegetable broth
2 cups diced onion (from 2 medium onions)
12 cups sliced button mushrooms
2 teaspoons dried dill or 2 tablespoons fresh
dill
1 tablespoon Hungarian paprika, or to taste
(can also use regular sweet paprika)
3 tablespoons soy sauce
(or gluten-free tamari)
2 cups rice milk
1/2 cup strained tomatoes
1 1/2 teaspoons sea salt, or to taste
Black pepper to taste

Optional:
1–2 tablespoons flour to thicken the soup

Garnish:
1 cup fresh minced parsley and tofu "sour
cream" (see the recipe on the next page)

Instructions

In a large soup pot:
- Place 1/4 cup of the vegetable broth and heat over medium heat

- Add the onion and a pinch of sea salt

- Cook and stir the onion for 5 to 10 minutes, or until the onions are tender

- Add the mushrooms, another pinch of sea salt and 1/4 cup of vegetable broth, and cook and stir for an additional 5 to 10 minutes, until the mushrooms have softened

- Stir in the dill, paprika, and soy sauce

- Add the remaining vegetable broth, rice milk, and strained tomatoes

- Cover the pot and reduce the heat to simmer on low for 20 minutes

- Add the sea salt and black pepper

- Optional: Add flour to 1/4 cup of cold water and stir until dissolved. Then add it to the soup and stir until thickened.

- Simmer for an additional 5 minutes

To serve:
- Serve hot, in decorative soup bowls, garnished with a dollop of tofu "sour cream" (see the recipe on the next page) and a sprinkling of fresh parsley.

---

jewishfoodhero.com

MUSHROOM SOUP WITH TOFU CREAM

Serves 8

(...continued)

Instructions

Make the tofu cream:

- Place all the ingredients in a blender or food processor and blend until smooth

Ingredients

Tofu "Sour Cream":
1 1/2 cups silken tofu
2 teaspoons lemon juice
Sea salt to taste

STUFFED CABBAGE

—

—

STUFFED CABBAGE

Serves 8 (makes 16 rolls)

This dish is as tasty and filling as traditional cabbage rolls, while being lighter and fresher in taste.
The rolls can be baked or made in a slow cooker. Double the recipe if you want to serve
it as leftovers the next day or if you would like guests to have more than two.
This dish is just as delicious served at room temperature as it is served hot.

Tools

Large pot
Tongs or large slotted spoon
Colander
Large skillet
Medium saucepan
Plate to assemble rolls
Glass baking dish (9 x 13 inch)
Parchment paper and aluminum foil

Optional:
Slow cooker

Ingredients

2 large heads green cabbage (with nice outer
leaves if possible) (you will need 16 nice large
outer cabbage leaves for the rolls)
1/4 cup vegetable broth, or more as needed
1 1/2 cups diced onion (from 1 large onion)
2 teaspoons minced garlic (from 4 cloves)
Sea salt to taste
3 cups coarsely grated or crumbled tempeh
2 tablespoons soy sauce
(or gluten-free tamari)
3/4 cup toasted pine nuts
3/4 cup dried currants or raisins
1 1/2 teaspoons caraway seeds
3 cups cooked pearled barley (from 3/4 cup
raw, prepared according to the package
directions, OR to make it gluten-free, use 3
cups cooked rice [from 1 cup raw])
Sea salt and black pepper to taste
A touch of olive oil cooking spray to grease
the casserole dish

Instructions

- Preheat the oven to 350 F

Parboil the cabbage:
- Carefully drop 1 head of cabbage into a large pot with boiling water

- After 5 minutes, remove the cabbage with tongs or a large slotted spoon, and place in a colander in the sink or over a large bowl to cool

- When cool enough to handle, carefully remove the outer leaves. You will need 16 leaves, so you can repeat this process and boil the same head of cabbage again to be able to remove more leaves, or you can boil the second head of cabbage if necessary

Make the filling:
- In a large skillet, heat the 1/4 cup of vegetable broth over medium heat

- Add the onion, garlic, and a pinch of sea salt.

- Cook and stir for 5 to 10 minutes, or until the onion is soft

- Stir in the tempeh and soy sauce, and cook for 15 minutes, adding more broth if needed to prevent sticking

- Add the pine nuts, currants, caraway seeds, and pearled barley

- Mix well and season with sea salt and pepper to taste

———

STUFFED CABBAGE

Serves 8 (makes 16 rolls)

(...continued)

Ingredients

For the sauce:
1/4 cup vegetable broth, plus more as needed
1 cup onion (from 1 onion)
2 cloves minced garlic
Salt to taste
2 7-ounce jars tomato paste
2 cups vegetable broth or water
2 cups strained tomatoes
2 teaspoons sugar
3 cups prepared sauerkraut
1 tablespoon Hungarian paprika
(or regular sweet paprika)
1–2 teaspoons sea salt, to taste
Black pepper to taste

Optional:
1/2 cup tofu "sour cream"
(see the recipe in Mushroom Soup)

Instructions

Make the sauce:
- Heat the 1/4 cup vegetable broth in a medium saucepan over medium heat
- Add the onion, garlic, and a pinch of sea salt
- Cook and stir for 5 to 10 minutes, or until the onion is tender
- Add the remaining sauce ingredients and cook for 20 minutes on low heat, covered, stirring occasionally

Make the cabbage rolls:
- To fill the cabbage leaves, place a cooked cabbage leaf on a plate
- Put a generous scoop of the tempeh-barley mixture on top, in the center of the leaf
- Roll up the leaf over the filling starting from the bottom, then fold in each side, and lastly the top, tucking the seam underneath
- Repeat with the remaining leaves until you have 16 nicely filled cabbage rolls

—

STUFFED CABBAGE

Serves 8 (makes 16 rolls)

(...continued)

Instructions

Assemble and bake:
If using a slow cooker: Cook the rolls in the sauce on low for 8 hours or until desired doneness.

- Prepare the casserole dish by lightly oiling it with the olive oil

- Put down enough sauce to cover the bottom of the dish

- Place the stuffed cabbage rolls on top of the sauce

- Cover the cabbage rolls with the remaining sauce

- Cover the casserole with a sheet of parchment paper and then with a sheet of aluminum foil

- Bake for 1 hour

- After 1 hour, check the cabbage rolls, add a little water if they have started to dry out

- Bake for an additional 15 minutes, until they are tender when pierced

To serve:
- Serve family style at the table, hot or at room temperature

---

Side

PICKLED BEETS

—

—

PICKLED BEETS

Serves 8

Make this dish at least two days prior to serving, and your guests will be delighted with your lovely homemade pickled beets! Consider making extra if you love pickled beets (they are that delicious). This is a fun activity to do with children who are ages 5 and up.

Tools

Large pot
Small saucepan
Whisk
Large glass bowl
Ball canning jars (or another canning jar)

Optional:
Small decorative bowls

Ingredients

8 large beets
1 cup rice vinegar
1 cup white wine vinegar
2 teaspoons sea salt
1/2 cup sugar
2 cups red onion, sliced into 1/4-inch rings
(from 2 medium onions)

Instructions

Cook the beets:
- Place the beets in a large pot and cover them with water
- Bring to a boil, then reduce the heat to simmer on low for 1 hour, until fork-tender

Meanwhile, quick pickle the onions:
- Prepare the brine for the onions by placing the rice vinegar, white wine vinegar, sea salt, and sugar in a small saucepan
- Warm on low heat until the sugar dissolves, whisking lightly
- Place the red onions in a large glass bowl and pour the vinegar mixture over them
- Set aside
- When the beets have finished cooking, run them under cold water until they are cool enough to handle
- Rub the skins off with your fingers

Assemble the dish:
- Slice the cooked beets into 1/4-inch rounds
- Combine the beets with the red onion-vinegar mixture
- Refrigerate in glass containers or canning jars for about 2 days prior to serving, to give them time to marinate

To serve:
- Serve on your table right from the canning jars or in small decorative bowls

—

Side

APPLE-CUCUMBER SALAD

—

—

jewishfoodhero.com

APPLE-CUCUMBER SALAD

Serves 8

This is the Korean-inspired salad! Refreshing, delicious, and crunchy, it adds color and
brightness to your holiday meal. The creamy dressing can be prepared two ways:
simple for the kids or with a horseradish twist for the grown-ups.

Tools

Food processor
Large salad bowl
Blender
Tongs

Ingredients

12 cups sliced red apples, cored but not peeled
(from 6 medium apples)
8 cups sliced English cucumbers
(from 2 cucumbers)
1 cup thinly sliced red onion (from 1 onion)

Dressing:
2 cups silken tofu
1/4 cup rice vinegar (or lemon juice)
1/4 cup chopped white onion (from 1/4 onion)
1 teaspoon sea salt, or more to taste

For adults:
Add 2 tablespoons prepared horseradish

Garnish:
2 cups dehydrated no-sugar-added apple
chips, or more if desired

Instructions

Prepare the salad:
- Using the thin slicing blade on the food processor,
  slice the apples and cucumbers

- Place the apples and cucumbers in a large bowl

Make the dressing:
- Place all the dressing ingredients in a blender or food
  processor, and blend until smooth

- Pour the dressing over the salad and toss with a pair
  of tongs

Garnish and serve the salad:
- Lightly toss the salad with the apple chips (add at the
  last minute so as to retain their crunchy texture)

- Serve family style at the table

FLODNI PARFAIT

—

—

FLODNI PARFAIT

Serves 8

Flodni is an iconic Hungarian dessert. This version has been lightened up and includes
the 5 following layers: whole-grain cereals, poppy and chia seeds, apples, prunes or
plum jam, and walnut maple syrup. Children can help assemble these parfait desserts
after all the layers have been already cooked and prepared.

Tools

Medium glass bowl
Microplane zester
Medium airtight container
(for the pudding layer)
3 small saucepans
Food processor or potato masher
Parfait glasses, wine glasses, or martini
glasses

Ingredients

Crunchy layer:
2 cups crushed brown rice crispy cereal
(measure after crushing in a mini food
processor—you will need to start out with
about 4 cups cereal)
2 cups Ezekiel (or Grape-Nuts) cereal

Optional:
1 tablespoon unrefined sugar

Chia/poppy seed pudding layer:
1/3 cup chia seeds
2 cups rice milk
2 tablespoons maple syrup
2 tablespoons poppy seeds
2 teaspoons all-natural vanilla extract
1 tablespoon fresh lemon zest
Pinch sea salt

Instructions

Make the crunchy layer:
• Place all the ingredients for this layer in a medium
glass bowl, and stir and crush

Make the chia/poppy seed pudding layer:
• Place all the ingredients for this layer together in a
medium airtight container, cover and refrigerate for
several hours until thickened

Make the walnut layer:
• Place all the ingredients for this layer in a small
saucepan and warm over medium-low heat for about
5 minutes, or until slightly thickened and bubbly

• Remove from the heat to cool

Make the apple layer:
• Place all the ingredients for this layer in a small
saucepan, and bring to a gentle boil over medium heat

• Reduce the heat to low and simmer for 5 to 10 minutes,
or until thickened to the consistency of apple pie filling

• Remove from the heat to cool at room temperature,
then chill in the refrigerator for at least an hour
before using

—

FLODNI PARFAIT

Serves 8

(...continued)

Ingredients

Walnut layer:
1 1/2 cups ground walnuts
1/2 cup maple syrup (or your favorite honey)
1/2 cup raisins or dried currants
1 teaspoon cinnamon
2 teaspoons all-natural vanilla extract

Apple layer:
3 cups cored and diced red apples
(with the skin) (from 3 medium apples)
1 cup apple juice
2 teaspoons cornstarch dissolved in a little of
the apple juice
Pinch sea salt

Optional:
2 teaspoons sugar

Plum/prune jam layer:*
1 1/2 cups prunes
2 cups water
Pinch sea salt
**Or skip making this and use 2 cups prepared
plum jam.*

Garnish:
2 red apples with skin, sliced thin

Instructions

Make the plum/prune jam layer:
- Place all the ingredients for this layer in a small saucepan

- Bring to a boil over medium heat, then reduce the heat to simmer on low, covered, for about 15 minutes

- Mash the mixture with a potato masher to the desired consistency (or blend in a food processor). Be aware that jam continues to thicken and set as it cools.

- Cool thoroughly before using

Assemble the parfaits:
- Place a small amount of the crunchy mixture on the bottom of each parfait glass

- Top with a spoonful of the chia/poppy seed pudding

- Sprinkle more of the crunchy mixture on top of the pudding layer

- Spoon a layer of the walnut mixture on top of the crunchy layer

- Top with another layer of the crunchy mixture

- Place a spoonful of the apple mixture on top

- Top again with more of the crunchy mixture

- Top it off with a spoonful of the plum/prune jam

- Finish with a light sprinkle of the crunchy mixture

Garnish the parfaits:
- Thinly slice two red apples

- Fan out 3 slices, and place them on top of each parfait in a nice design (or stand them up, by sticking them slightly down into the top layer of the parfait)

—

—

SIMCHAT TORAH

—

www.jewishfoodhero.com

—

SIMCHAT TORAH

The Inspiration Behind This Menu

This menu was inspired by my first international work experience in 2005. It was in Chennai, India, where I was a volunteer with American Jewish World Service, working for an NGO that served homeless women experiencing mental illness.

During my time there, I lived in housing provided by the NGO; it was a vegetarian ashram devoted to energetic healing. Up to forty women would come to the ashram on a daily basis for classes.

These women would eat there too, and so every morning I would wake up to a bustling kitchen where women were busy making curries, dahls, rice, and desserts for the day. I fell in love with that kitchen and the food.

This menu offers healthy Indian food that you can enjoy all year round, and especially on Simchat Torah.

—

jewishfoodhero.com

MENU

—

APPETIZER

Spiced Apple Compote

MAIN DISH

Biryani Vegetable Rice

SIDE

Warm Cabbage Salad With Peanuts

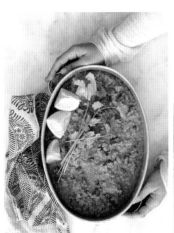

SIDE

Creamy Lentil Dahl

SIDE

Pickled Red Onions

DESSERT

Tapioca Pudding*

*This recipe can be prepared by children with adult supervision.

—

jewishfoodhero.com

Appetizer

SPICED APPLE COMPOTE

—

—

jewishfoodhero.com

SPICED APPLE COMPOTE

Serves 8

What a sweet treat to serve this delicious cooked fruit dish as a first course! It's naturally sweet, though if you like a sweeter taste, feel free to add a little sugar when cooking. Not to be mistaken as applesauce, this was probably a favorite of your grandmother's when she was younger. Regaining popularity, fruit compotes are as healthy as it gets when it comes to sweet dishes!

Instructions

In a large saucepan:

- Bring all the ingredients to a gentle simmer over medium-high heat

- Cover and reduce the heat to simmer on low for 25 minutes

- Check the liquid level while cooking and add a little more water or juice if needed

- If any cooking liquid remains after 25 minutes, remove the lid and increase the heat to reduce

To serve:

- Serve in small decorative bowls

Tools

Large saucepan
Small decorative bowls for serving

Ingredients

6 cups cored and diced red apples
(from 6 medium apples)
1 1/2 cups cored and diced pears
(from 2 medium pears)
1 cup unfiltered, unsweetened apple juice,
plus more as needed
2 teaspoons cinnamon
1/2 teaspoon nutmeg
1/2 teaspoon cloves
1/2 teaspoon cardamom

Optional:
1/2 cup dried currants

———

Main Dish

BIRYANI VEGETABLE RICE

—

—

BIRYANI VEGETABLE RICE

Serves 8

This flavorful rice is loaded with vegetables and warming spices.
Serve this warm garnished with crunchy cashews and fresh cilantro.

Tools

Large sauté pan
Large pot
Cooking oil
Deep (4 quart) covered baking dish
Fork
Large serving platter

Ingredients

1/4 cup vegetable broth for sautéing
(more as needed)
1 cup finely diced onion (from 1 medium onion)
1 teaspoon minced garlic
1 teaspoon minced ginger
1 cup cauliflower florets
(from 1 small head of cauliflower)
1 cup sliced carrots (from 3 medium carrots)
1 cup diced tomatoes (from 2 fresh tomatoes)
1 cup green beans, cut into 1-inch pieces
3 cups raw brown basmati rice, rinsed and drained
5 1/2 cups water
1/3 cup raisins

Spices:
2 bay leaves
2 teaspoons sea salt
2 teaspoons ground cinnamon
1/2 teaspoon ground cardamom
1/2 teaspoon ground cloves
1 teaspoon curry powder (or more if desired)
1/2 teaspoon ground coriander

Garnish:
1 cup no-salt dry-roasted cashews
1 cup fresh cilantro sprigs

Instructions

- Preheat the oven to 350 F

Cook the onion, garlic, and ginger:
- In a large sauté pan, heat the vegetable broth over medium-high heat

- Add the onion, garlic, and ginger

- Cook for 5 minutes, or until the onions are tender, stirring frequently

- Add a small amount of additional broth if needed

Add in the other prepped vegetables and spices:
- Add the cauliflower, carrots, tomatoes, green beans, and the spices (except for the bay leaves and salt)

- Cover and cook for another 5 minutes

Cook the rice:
- Place the rice, water, bay leaves, and sea salt in a large pot and bring to a boil over medium-high heat

Assemble the casserole and bake:
- Pour the hot rice mixture into a lightly oiled casserole

- Add the cooked vegetables and raisins to the rice and gently stir together to combine

- Cover and bake for 1 hour, or until the rice is tender

Prior to serving:
- Fluff the rice with a fork

Garnish and serve:
- Serve hot, on a large serving platter, garnished with chopped cashews and cilantro

---

Side

WARM CABBAGE SALAD WITH PEANUTS

—

—

WARM CABBAGE SALAD WITH PEANUTS

Serves 8

This cabbage dish has hints of flavorful cumin, ginger, and garlic with a garnish of peanuts and coconut. If you want a little more spiciness, add the optional mustard seeds and chilies.

Tools

Large glass bowl
Large skillet
Small glass bowl for toasted spices
Large serving bowl

Ingredients

8 cups of very thinly shredded green cabbage
(from 1 head cabbage)
2/3 cup coarsely shredded carrots
(from 2 medium carrots)
1 teaspoon sea salt, or to taste
1–2 tablespoons vegetable broth, as needed
1 teaspoon minced garlic (from about 2 cloves)
1 teaspoon minced, peeled ginger
(from 1 small chunk)
1/2 teaspoon turmeric
1/2 teaspoon ground cumin
Fresh lemon juice to taste

Optional:
2 teaspoons toasted mustard seeds
(makes it a little spicy)

Optional:
1 to 2 fresh green serrano chilies, stems
discarded (makes it a little spicy)

Garnish:
1/2 cup finely chopped peanuts
1/2 cup dried desiccated unsweetened
shredded or grated coconut
1 cup fresh cilantro

Instructions

Massage the prepped cabbage and carrots:
- Place the cabbage and carrots in a large glass bowl

- Massage the sea salt into the cabbage and carrots and set aside for 5 minutes to soften the cabbage and carrots before cooking

Dry roast the mustard seeds:
- If using the mustard seeds, heat a large skillet over medium heat

- Add the mustard seeds and stir for several minutes to dry roast them

- Set aside

Cook the aromatics and vegetables:
- Heat the vegetable broth in the same skillet over medium heat

- Add the garlic and ginger and sauté for a few minutes

- Add the salted cabbage and carrots, optional mustard seeds if using, turmeric, and ground cumin

- Cook and stir for 3 to 5 minutes (longer if you want the vegetables more cooked and less crunchy)

- Add fresh lemon juice to taste

To serve:
- Serve hot, room temperature, or chilled, family style in a large serving bowl

---

Side

CREAMY LENTIL DAHL

—

—

CREAMY LENTIL DAHL

Serves 8

This comforting bean dish is perfect served as a side to the Biryani Vegetable Rice.
You can partially mash either some of it or most of it, depending how creamy you want it.

Tools

Large saucepan
Medium skillet
Potato masher or immersion blender
Individual bowls for serving

Ingredients

3 1/2 cups uncooked red lentils, rinsed and drained
9 cups water
1/4 cup vegetable broth for sautéing, or more as needed
4 cups finely diced onion (from 4 medium onions)
1 1/2 tablespoons minced ginger
(from 1 large chunk)
1 1/2 tablespoons minced garlic
4 cups diced tomatoes
(from 8 medium tomatoes) OR tomato puree
1 1/2 tablespoons ground cumin
4 1/2 cups unsweetened rice milk
(or other non-dairy milk)
1 teaspoon sea salt, or to taste

Garnish:
1 cup fresh cilantro sprigs
8 lemon wedges

Instructions

Cook the lentils:
- Place lentils in a large saucepan with water
- Bring to a boil uncovered
- Reduce the heat to simmer on low for 30 minutes or until the lentils are tender

Meanwhile, make the tomato sauce:
- In a medium skillet, heat the 1/4 cup vegetable broth over medium heat
- Add the onion, ginger, and garlic
- Cook for 10 minutes, or until tender, stirring often
- Add small amounts of additional broth if needed to prevent sticking
- Add the tomatoes and cumin, and cook for another 10 minutes

Add the sauce to the lentils and continue to cook:
- Pour the sauce over the cooked lentils in the large saucepan
- Add the rice milk
- Bring to a boil over medium-high heat
- Reduce the heat to simmer on low, covered, for 20 minutes
- Add the sea salt and simmer for 5 more minutes
- Adjust seasoning to taste

CREAMY LENTIL DAHL

Serves 8

(...continued)

Puree the dish:

- Use a potato masher or immersion blender to partially mash/puree half of the lentils

Garnish and serve:

- Serve hot, over rice, garnished with fresh cilantro and a squeeze of fresh lemon juice

—

PICKLED RED ONIONS

—

—

PICKLED RED ONIONS

Serves 8

Pickles are an essential component to any Indian meal.
They add flavor, texture, variety, and also help to digest heavier stews and bean dishes.

Instructions

In a medium glass bowl:

• Place all the ingredients and mix well

• Let sit for 2 hours to marinate, massaging occasionally to break down the onions

To store:

• Transfer to a glass jar to store in the refrigerator for up to a week

To serve:

• Serve alongside the savory meal of your choice, in several small decorative bowls placed along the table

Tools

Medium glass bowl
Glass jar
(clean and preferably boiled to sterilize)
Several small decorative bowls for serving

Ingredients

2 cups red onion (from 2 medium onions),
thinly sliced into half moons
1/2 cup lime juice (from about 2 limes)
1/2 cup apple cider vinegar
2 teaspoons sea salt
1 teaspoon sugar
1 teaspoon Indian red chili powder

Optional:
1 tablespoon minced green chilies

———

jewishfoodhero.com

Dessert

TAPIOCA PUDDING

—

—

jewishfoodhero.com

TAPIOCA PUDDING

Serves 8

Tapioca pudding is always a comforting favorite for dessert. Children will love to see the tapioca pearls "grow" as they soak. The pudding itself is a pure white color. When garnished with edible flowers, crushed pistachios, and a sprinkle of warming spices, the pudding is simply beautiful. You can also serve this as a dessert during Passover by using almond milk instead of rice milk.

Tools

Medium strainer
Medium saucepan
Individual dessert bowls for serving

Ingredients

1 cup large tapioca pearls
3 cups rice milk or unsweetened almond milk
3 cups coconut milk
(Use the unsweetened variety sold in cartons. Do <u>not</u> use canned coconut milk or cream.)
1/2 cup sugar

Garnish:
8 pieces edible flowers
(such as pansies or rose petals)
1/2 cup ground pistachios
Sprinkle of cinnamon or cardamom

Instructions

Prep and cook the tapioca pearls:
- Rinse the tapioca pearls in a strainer to remove the excess starch

- In a medium saucepan, place 2 cups of the rice milk and 2 cups of the coconut milk

- Bring the milk mixture to a boil

- Stir in the tapioca pearls

- Reduce the heat to simmer on low, partially covered, for 20 minutes, or until the tapioca pearls are soft and translucent

- Stir occasionally during cooking

Finish making the pudding:
- In the same saucepan, add the remaining 1 cup of rice milk, 1 cup of coconut milk, and the sugar

- Cook for an additional 10 minutes

Chill the pudding:
- Cool the pudding at room temperature for 30 minutes, then refrigerate for at least 1 hour to set

Garnish and serve:
- When ready to serve, place in individual dessert bowls

- Serve garnished with flowers, pistachios, and a sprinkle of cardamom and/or cinnamon

---

—

CHANUKAH

—

—

CHANUKAH

The Inspiration Behind This Menu

As a child, my family would celebrate Chanukah by going to the party held at the only synagogue in the small town of Waterville, Maine.

The Chanukah party was in the synagogue's basement, and I remember walking into the kitchen there with my mother and seeing all the women in the community cooking for the party. There were blue streamers hung from the ceiling, and paper cutouts of dreidels and menorahs on the walls. No matter how cold it was outside, the basement was always toasty and warm.

This Chanukah menu is food revisionist history. It evokes my adolescent desires for what I wish had been served at those parties—combined with my current knowledge of plant-based food.

It's festive and fresh food that is healthy and nourishing, and perfect for your own Chanukah celebration.

—

MENU

—

APPETIZER
Banana-Mango Smoothie*

MAIN DISH
*Latkes with Chili Cream
and Applesauce*

SIDE
Bean Salsa Salad With Corn

SIDE
Spiced Acorn Squash

DESSERT
Strawberry-Glazed Sufganiyot

*This recipe can be prepared by children with adult supervision.

—

jewishfoodhero.com

BANANA-MANGO SMOOTHIE

—

—

BANANA-MANGO SMOOTHIE

Makes 8 cups

This light, creamy, and refreshing smoothie tastes delicious as a starter.
You may even want to make a double batch, as it pairs well with the sufganiyot.

Instructions

In a blender:

- Combine all the ingredients and blend until smooth and creamy

To serve:

- Serve in shooters or small cups

Tools

High-powered blender
Small serving cups or shooters

Ingredients

4 cups non-dairy milk
2 cups frozen banana slices
(from 4 medium bananas)
2 cups frozen mangoes (from 2 medium
mangoes), OR one 15-ounce bag of
frozen mangoes
2 teaspoons all-natural vanilla extract
1 teaspoon ground cinnamon

LATKES WITH CHILI CREAM AND APPLESAUCE

—

—

LATKES WITH CHILI CREAM AND APPLESAUCE

Makes 20–24 latkes

These latkes are hearty and crispy. Using minimal oil, they're a tasty and healthy option for your holiday menu (and for the rest of the year too). Each latke can be served with your toppings of choice: chili "sour cream" and/or cinnamon applesauce.

Tools

Box grater
Large mixing bowl
2 baking sheets
Parchment paper
Cooking oil spray
Spatula
Large platter for serving

Ingredients

14 cups peeled, shredded white potatoes
(from about 8 medium potatoes)
2 cups cooked yam puree
(from 1 medium yam, peeled and steamed)
1/4 cup low-fat, non-dairy milk
1 1/3 cups all-purpose flour, or gluten-free
all-purpose flour
3 teaspoons sea salt
1 teaspoon baking powder

Instructions

- Preheat the oven to 350 F

Assemble the latke mixture and bake:

- Place all the prepped ingredients in a large mixing bowl and stir to combine
- Line a baking sheet with parchment paper, and lightly spray with the cooking spray
- Place 1/2 cup of the latke mixture on the baking sheet
- Flatten the latke with your hands and form it into an even circle
- Repeat until you have enough latkes to fill the baking sheet
- Lightly mist the formed latkes with the cooking oil spray
- Bake for 25 minutes
- Very carefully, flip the latkes and mist again with the cooking oil spray
- Bake for another 15 minutes
- Repeat with the remaining latke mixture until you use all of it

To serve and store:

- Keep the cooked latkes warm in the oven until ready to serve
- Serve on a large platter alongside cinnamon applesauce and chili "sour cream" (recipes on the next pages)
- If you have leftovers, place them covered in the refrigerator—they taste delicious cold

CINNAMON APPLESAUCE

Makes 3 cups

(...continued)

Tools

Large saucepan
Potato masher (or food processor)
Medium serving bowl

Ingredients

12 cups cored, peeled, and diced apples
(from about 12 medium apples)
1 1/2 cups apple juice
1 teaspoon sea salt
1/4 cup plus 2 tablespoons raw sugar or maple
syrup
1 1/4 teaspoons cinnamon

Instructions

In a large sauce pan:
- Place all the ingredients, and bring to a gentle boil over medium heat
- Reduce the heat to low, and simmer covered for 25 minutes
- Partially mash the apples or puree them smooth

To serve:
- Place in a medium serving bowl, and serve at the temperature of your choice

—

CHILI "SOUR CREAM"

Makes 3 cups

(...continued)

Instructions

In a blender or food processor:

- Puree all the ingredients until smooth

Garnish and serve:

- Top with a sprinkling of paprika and chopped peppers

Tools

Blender or food processor
Medium serving bowl

Ingredients

3 cups soft silken tofu

3 tablespoons fresh lemon juice

3 tablespoons sugar

2 teaspoons salt

1–2 chopped fresh cayenne peppers, to taste

Optional garnish:
Sweet paprika and chopped cayenne pepper

—

BEAN SALSA SALAD WITH CORN

—

—

BEAN SALSA SALAD WITH CORN

Serves 8

This colorful salad is a wonderful, light addition to the more filling holiday fare.
It's just as pretty to look at as it is refreshing to eat.

Tools

Small bowl
Medium bowl
Large salad bowl
Colander

Optional:
Juicer

Ingredients

1 cup finely chopped shallots
(from 4 medium shallots)
4 teaspoons finely chopped garlic (from 8 cloves)
3 cups de-seeded and diced tomatoes
(from 6 tomatoes)
5 cups lettuce, cut into small strips
(from 1 medium head of lettuce)
3 cups cubed cucumbers
(from 2 medium cucumbers)
2 cups diced orange bell peppers
(from 2 peppers) (if you don't like peppers,
you can replace them with another colorful
vegetable of your choice or simply add more
tomatoes and cucumbers)
2 14-ounce cans of kidney beans
2–3 ears of corn or one 14-ounce can of corn

Garnish:
Fresh chopped cilantro

Dressing:
3/4 cup plus 2 tablespoons lime juice
(from about 7 limes)
3/4 teaspoon salt
1/2 teaspoon pepper
1/2 teaspoon cumin
1 teaspoon apple cider vinegar

Instructions

Juice the lime and assemble the salsa:

- In a small bowl juice the lime

- In a medium bowl, place the prepped shallots, garlic, and tomatoes

- Add salt, pepper, and cumin to the mixture, and adjust seasoning to taste

- Pour most of the lime juice over the mixture, stir well, and set aside to let marinate for up to 1 hour

- Save a little of the lime juice in case you want to add more to the salad at the end

Assemble the salad:

- Put the prepped lettuce strips, cucumbers, and bell peppers in a large salad bowl

- Drain the beans and corn if using canned, rinse in a colander, and add to the salad bowl

- Add the marinated salsa mixture to the salad bowl

- Using your hands, mix gently

- Taste and add more lime juice if desired

Garnish and serve:

- Garnish with finely chopped cilantro just before serving

—

SPICED ACORN SQUASH

—

—

SPICED ACORN SQUASH

Serves 8

This festive squash dish has it all: It's sweet, spicy, savory, and incredibly satisfying.
Feel free to vary the type of squash and how much spice you use to your taste.

Tools

2 baking trays
Small bowl
Glass jar with cover, for mixing
Aluminum foil
Large serving platter

Ingredients

4 acorn squash
(or other varieties of green-skinned winter
squash such as buttercup or kabocha squash)

Spice marinade:
1 tablespoon chili powder
1 tablespoon ground cumin
1 tablespoon paprika
2 teaspoons oregano
1 teaspoon salt
1 teaspoon cinnamon
2 cups vegetable broth
1 teaspoon minced fresh garlic (from 2 cloves)

Instructions

• Preheat the oven to 350 F

Prepare the acorn squash:
• Cut the squash lengthwise and de-seed

• Place on 2 baking trays and set aside

Make the spice marinade:
• Mix the chili powder, cumin, paprika, oregano,
  salt, and cinnamon together in a small bowl

• Place vegetable broth in a glass mixing jar

• Add the desired amount of the powdered spice mix to
  the broth (half of the mixture if you like less spice and
  all if you like a powerful taste). Add the prepared garlic,
  and close the jar with the lid.

• Shake vigorously to combine

Assemble and bake the squash:
• Pour the spice liquid over the acorn squash, making
  sure each one is covered with 1 inch of liquid

• If you want to prepare some of the squash spice-free,
  just add plain vegetable broth to the acorn squash,
  making sure each one is covered with 1 inch of liquid

• Cover with aluminum foil, and bake for 30 minutes

• Uncover and bake for 15 more minutes, or until the
  squash is tender

To serve:
• Transfer to a serving platter, and serve warm

—

Dessert

STRAWBERRY-GLAZED SUFGANIYOT

—

—

STRAWBERRY-GLAZED SUFGANIYOT

Makes 15

Sufganiyot are iconic for Chanukah. I wanted to make a version that's better for you than the traditional deep-fried ones. These easy baked doughnuts avoid all the traditional mess of deep-frying, but are just as delicious. Glistening with strawberry glaze, these doughnuts will delight you and your guests.

Tools

Medium mixing bowl
Whisk
Large mixing bowl
1 doughnut pan (this is an absolute requirement to bake these doughnuts)
Cooking oil spray
Small saucepan
Dessert platter for serving

Ingredients

Dry ingredients:
1 1/2 cups all-purpose flour
(or gluten-free all-purpose baking flour)
3/4 cup raw sugar
1 1/4 teaspoons baking powder
1 teaspoon baking soda
1/2 teaspoon sea salt
1 teaspoon cinnamon

Wet ingredients:
3/4 cup coconut milk
(can also use almond milk or soy milk)
1/4 cup safflower oil
1/2 cup applesauce
1 1/2 teaspoons all-natural vanilla extract
3/4 teaspoon apple cider vinegar
3/4 cup all-fruit strawberry jam

Instructions

- Preheat the oven to 350 F

Prepare the dry ingredients:
- In a medium mixing bowl, whisk together all the dry ingredients

Prepare the wet ingredients:
- In a large mixing bowl, combine the coconut milk, 1/4 cup safflower oil, 1/2 cup applesauce, vanilla extract, and apple cider vinegar

Combine the two mixtures and bake:
- Add the dry mixture to the wet and mix quickly (do not overmix)

- Spray the doughnut pan lightly with cooking oil spray

- Fill each doughnut cavity until 2/3 full (and not more)

- Bake for 12 to 15 minutes until the doughnuts spring back to the touch

- Allow to cool

- Remove the doughnuts from the pan by inverting it

- Keep them warm in the oven until ready to serve

While the sufganiyot bake:
- Warm the strawberry jam in a small saucepan for a few minutes

- Glaze the doughnut tops with the all-fruit jam just before serving

To serve:
- Arrange on a dessert platter, and serve the same day

———

—

TU B'SHVAT

—

—

TU B'SHVAT

The Inspiration Behind This Menu

In 2013, I had the good fortune to visit the tropical Singapore Botanical Gardens. It is one of three gardens worldwide and the only tropical garden to be honored as a UNESCO World Heritage Site.

My favorite part of the visit was the National Orchid Garden. It's located on a hilly three-hectare site that showcases a collection of more than 1,000 species and 2,000 hybrids of orchids.

However, we spent most of our visit at the Jacob Ballas Children's Garden, which is Asia's first garden dedicated solely to children. The Children's Garden was named after its main donor, Jacob Ballas, a Jewish-Singaporean philanthropist who died in 2004. It aims to provide a place for children to learn, play, and explore amidst nature through engaging their five senses (especially smell and touch).

After our visit, I kept daydreaming about having a Tu B'Shvat picnic at the garden. I created a menu I thought would be perfect for this fantasy picnic.

—

Energetic Theme: *Grow*

MENU

—

APPETIZER

Mint Citrus Plate

MAIN DISH

Gong Bao Garbanzo Beans
With Soba Noodles

SIDE

Tamari-Maple Cabbage Salad

SIDE

Green Tea Smoothie With Ginger

DESSERT

Date Balls (Sweet and Spicy Versions)*

*This recipe can be prepared by children with adult supervision.

—

jewishfoodhero.com

Appetizer

MINT CITRUS PLATE

—

—

MINT CITRUS PLATE

Serves 8

This light appetizer will go over well with both adults and children. The sweetness of the oranges is enhanced by the addition of sea salt and balsamic vinegar.

Tools

Medium bowl
Serving platter

Ingredients

1 1/2 cups thinly sliced fennel
(from 1 large head)
1/2 teaspoon sea salt
2 teaspoons lemon juice
5 medium oranges, for sectioning
4 medium grapefruits, for sectioning
1/2 teaspoon sea salt
1 1/2 tablespoons balsamic vinegar
(a thick variety can be nice)

Garnish:
3 tablespoons finely sliced mint leaves
(or more), from 1 small bunch

Instructions

In a medium bowl:

- Place the prepared fennel and add the sea salt and lemon juice

- Gently massage the sea salt and lemon juice into the sliced fennel, and set aside to marinate while preparing the other elements of the salad

Prepare the citrus fruits, and assemble the salad:

- Remove the skin and outer membrane from the oranges and the grapefruit

- Slice the oranges into 1/4-inch thick round slices

- Arrange the citrus on a serving platter and lightly sprinkle to taste with the sea salt

- Drizzle evenly to taste with the balsamic vinegar

- Drain the fennel and sprinkle over the top of the salad

Chill, garnish, and serve:

- Chill the platter for 1 hour before serving

- When ready, take out of the refrigerator and garnish with the mint leaves

———

GONG BAO GARBANZO BEANS WITH SOBA NOODLES

—

—

GONG BAO GARBANZO BEANS WITH SOBA NOODLES

Serves 8

Gong Bao is traditionally a spicy dish combining Sichuan peppercorns and dried red chilies. This version is family friendly without all the spiciness for children or for anyone who enjoys milder dishes. The recipe has the flavorful additions of kale and squash, and is served over soba noodles.

Tools

Large pot
Slotted spoon
Colander or strainer
Medium bowl
2 small bowls
Large skillet
Small skillet
Food processor (if using the chilies)
Large serving platter

Ingredients

4 1/2 cups cubed butternut squash (either fresh or packaged) (from 1 butternut squash)
2 bunches kale (or another green leafy vegetable), de-stemmed and cut or ripped into bite-size pieces
1 pound soba noodles or gluten-free spaghetti
1 tablespoon, or to taste, of soy sauce or gluten-free tamari

Instructions

Boil the squash, the kale, and the soba noodles:
- Bring a large pot of water to a boil over high heat

- Drop the cubed butternut squash into the boiling water

- Cook for 2 minutes

- Remove with a slotted spoon

- Place in a colander to cool and drain

- Repeat the same process with the kale

- Cook the soba noodles in the same water, according to package directions

When the noodles are cooked:
- Drain in a colander

- Put back into the pot

- Toss the cooked and drained noodles with 1 tablespoon of soy sauce

- Cover and set aside

Make the sauce for everyone in a small bowl:
- Combine the raw sugar, soy sauce, and rice vinegar

- Set aside

—

GONG BAO GARBANZO BEANS WITH SOBA NOODLES

Serves 8

(...continued)

Ingredients

Sauce for everyone:

1/4 cup raw sugar or maple syrup

1/4 cup soy sauce

3 tablespoons rice vinegar

3/4 cup vegetable broth (or water)

2 teaspoons minced garlic (from 2 cloves)

2 teaspoons minced, peeled fresh ginger

4 cups cooked garbanzo beans
(if using canned, drained and rinsed)

6 scallion stems (from 1 bunch of scallions),
sliced into 1/4-inch pieces

3 teaspoons cornstarch or arrowroot

2 tablespoons water

Optional spices:

2 dried red chilies, broken with seeds
removed and discarded

1 teaspoon Sichuan peppercorns

Instructions

Finish cooking the vegetables in the sauce:

- Heat the vegetable broth over medium-high heat

- Add the garlic and ginger

- Cook and stir for 5 minutes

- Add the cooked squash, kale, garbanzo beans, and scallions

- Stir briefly, then add the sauce

- Cover and let steam for 5 minutes, or until the kale and butternut squash have softened

- Add additional broth if needed to prevent sticking

Meanwhile, in a small bowl:

- Combine the cornstarch with 2 tablespoons of cold water

- Stir to combine

Thicken the vegetable/sauce mixture:

- Add cornstarch mixture to the cooking vegetables and garbanzo beans, and stir until the sauce thickens slightly

If adding the optional chilies and Sichuan peppercorns:

- Heat a small skillet over medium heat, add the chilies and peppercorns, and cook, stirring constantly, for a few minutes. Do not over-roast.

- Use the chilies as they are, or pulse them in a food processor

- Add the spices to the vegetable-bean mixture

- Adjust seasonings to taste

To serve:

- While still hot, make a bed of the soba noodles on a large serving platter

- Pour the sauce and vegetables over the noodles, and serve immediately

———

TAMARI-MAPLE CABBAGE SALAD

—

—

TAMARI-MAPLE CABBAGE SALAD

Serves 8

This crunchy and colorful coleslaw makes a striking presentation, and is an easy-to-prepare side dish.

Instructions

In a large bowl:

- Combine all of the prepared salad ingredients

Marinate the salad:

- Pour the prepared Tamari Maple Dressing (recipe on the next page) over the top of the salad mixture and massage by hand to work the dressing into the vegetables

- Serve after marinating in the refrigerator for two hours

Tools

Large salad bowl

Ingredients

6 cups shredded green cabbage (or napa cabbage) (from 1 medium head of cabbage)
2 cups shredded red cabbage
(from 1 small cabbage)
2 cups julienned or coarsely shredded carrots
(from 6 medium carrots)

Optional:
1 cup julienned scallions
(from 1 bunch scallions)

———

jewishfoodhero.com

TAMARI MAPLE DRESSING

Serves 8

(...continued)

Tools

Small saucepan (2 quart)
Whisk

Ingredients

1/4 cup vegetable broth (or water)
1 tablespoon minced ginger
(from 1-inch segment)
2 teaspoons minced garlic
(from 2 medium cloves)
3 tablespoons maple syrup
(or unrefined sugar)
1/4 cup soy sauce or gluten-free tamari, or
more to taste
1/2 cup fresh orange juice
(from 2 medium oranges)
1/2 cup rice vinegar

Instructions

In a small saucepan:
- Heat the vegetable broth

- Add the ginger and garlic

- Cook and stir for 5 minutes

- Add the raw sugar and soy sauce

- Cook for a few more minutes until the sugar has dissolved

- Turn off the heat

- Add the orange juice and rice vinegar

- Whisk well, and let cool

To serve:
- Pour over salad and toss to combine

GREEN TEA SMOOTHIE WITH GINGER

—

—

GREEN TEA SMOOTHIE WITH GINGER

Serves 8

The flavors of the East combine beautifully in this refreshing smoothie.

Instructions

In a blender:

- Place all the prepared ingredients in the blender and puree until smooth and creamy in consistency

- Serve in shooters or small glasses

Tools

Blender
Small serving glasses or shooters

Ingredients

3 cups brewed and cooled green tea
(from 3 green tea bags and 3 cups of hot water)
5 cups frozen peaches
2 cups vanilla non-dairy yogurt
4–5 pitted dates
(soaked in water for 10 minutes, then drained)
2 teaspoons pure vanilla extract
2 teaspoons grated fresh ginger root

—

jewishfoodhero.com

TU B'SHVAT

Dessert

DATE BALLS

—

—

jewishfoodhero.com

DATE BALLS (SPICY VERSION)

Serves 8

These little treats are so easy to make. The added chilies are for anyone who enjoys a little spice. This recipe was inspired by a treat that can be found at any Vietnamese market in Ho Chi Minh City.

Instructions

In a food processor:

- Place the almonds and sea salt, and pulse until finely ground

- Add the dates and dried red chili pepper

- If the mixture seems too dry, add a few drops of water or orange juice until it sticks together when you squeeze it

Form the date balls:

- Form 1 rounded tablespoon of the mixture into a small ball

- Roll in the toasted sesame seeds

To serve:

- Arrange the date balls on a decorative dessert platter

Tools

Food processor
Tablespoon
Dessert platter for serving

Ingredients

1/2 cup almonds
1/8 tablespoon sea salt
2 cups pitted dates, roughly chopped
(from about 16 dates)
1 teaspoon dried red chili pepper, or to taste

Coating:
Toasted sesame seeds

Optional:
A few drops of water or orange juice

———

jewishfoodhero.com

DATE BALLS (SWEET VERSION)

Serves 8

Your children will love this sweet version of the date balls,
and they'll enjoy helping to make them as well!

Instructions

In a food processor:

- Place the almonds and sea salt, and pulse until finely ground

- Add the dates and vanilla extract

- If the mixture seems too dry, add a few drops of water or orange juice until it sticks together when you squeeze it

Form the date balls:

- Form 1 rounded tablespoon of the mixture into a small ball

- Roll in the crushed toasted almonds

- Serve in a way that you think is pretty

Tools

Food processor
Tablespoon
Dessert platter for serving

Ingredients

1/2 cup almonds
Pinch sea salt
2 cups pitted dates, roughly chopped
(from about 16 dates)
1 1/2 teaspoons vanilla extract

Coating:
Crushed toasted almonds

Optional:
A few drops of water or orange juice

———

jewishfoodhero.com

—

PURIM

—

PURIM

The Inspiration Behind This Menu

This menu was inspired by the question: "Was Queen Esther on a diet?"

I find the Talmudic story of Queen Esther's vegetarianism compelling and inspiring. (It appears in some manuscripts of Megillah 13b.) Esther needed to keep the laws of kashrut while hiding her Jewish heritage, so vegetarianism might have been her perfect solution.

So to answer my own question, Queen Esther was probably not on a diet, but maybe she was on a mission. Based on what we know today, it's highly possible that her switch to eating more fruits, vegetables, tubers, legumes, and whole grains impacted how she felt in her body and in the world.

Eating plant-based food might have stabilized her mood and energy levels throughout the day, and given her a taste of her own courage—showing her that she had the capacity to step outside of the mainstream (it's hard not to eat what everyone else is eating!).

Esther's courage and fortitude ultimately saved the Jews of Persia, and bequeathed us one of the most enjoyable holidays of the year. This Purim, you can highlight plant-based foods in honor of this story and in honor of your own health.

—

jewishfoodhero.com

MENU

—

APPETIZER
Pureed Carrot Soup

MAIN DISH
Choreschte Lape

SIDE
Persian Rice With Currants

SIDE
Cucumber Salad
With Creamy Dressing

DESSERT
Hamantaschen Cookies*

*This recipe can be prepared by children with adult supervision.

—

jewishfoodhero.com

Appetizer

PUREED CARROT SOUP

—

—

PUREED CARROT SOUP

Serves 8

This is an elegant soup that is easy to prepare and
serves as the first course of your Persian Purim menu.

Tools

Medium pot and steamer basket, if using
fresh squash
Medium bowl, if using fresh squash
Large soup pot
Immersion blender
Individual soup bowls for serving

Ingredients

1 15-ounce can butternut squash puree,
OR 1 medium butternut squash, peeled,
cubed, steamed, and mashed
8 cups vegetable broth (or water)
1 cup yellow or white onion, diced
(from 1 medium onion)
1 teaspoon sea salt, or to taste
4 cups peeled and chopped carrots
(from 7 medium carrots)
2 cups unsweetened low-fat rice milk
(or water)
2 tablespoons raw white rice
(this makes the soup creamy)
Freshly ground black pepper, to taste

Garnish:
1/4 cup chopped fresh mint

Instructions

Prepare the butternut squash puree, if using fresh:
- Peel, cube, and steam the butternut squash until
  fork-tender

- Set aside to cool in a medium bowl

In a large soup pot:
- Heat 1/2 cup of the vegetable broth (or water) over
  medium heat

- Add the onion and a pinch of the sea salt

- Cook and stir for 5 minutes, until the onions are soft

- Add the carrots and another splash of vegetable broth

- Cook and stir for 5 more minutes

- Add the rice milk, the 2 tablespoons of rice, and enough
  of the vegetable broth (or water) so that the liquid just
  barely covers the vegetables

- Bring to a boil over medium-high heat

- Cover and reduce the heat to simmer on low for 25
  minutes, or until the carrots are tender

Add the butternut squash puree and blend:
- Stir in the butternut squash puree

- Puree the soup with an immersion blender to achieve
  a creamy, smooth consistency

- Add the remaining sea salt and black pepper to taste

- Simmer for 5 more minutes

- Adjust seasonings to taste

To serve:
- Ladle the hot soup into individual soup bowls,
  and garnish with a sprinkling of fresh mint

Main Dish

CHORESCHTE LAPE

—

—

CHORESCHTE LAPE

Serves 8

This classic Persian stew combines sweet and savory seasonings for a rich depth of flavor. You can use yellow split peas or red lentils for this dish. Serve this dish over Persian rice (the following recipe).

Tools

Large pot
Large serving bowl

Ingredients

6 cups vegetable broth (or water)
1 cup chopped onion (from 1 large onion)
1 1/2 teaspoons minced garlic (from 3 cloves)
1 1/2 teaspoons sea salt, or to taste
7 cups baby bella mushrooms, cleaned and sliced
4 ounces tomato paste
1 cup canned, fire-roasted diced tomatoes (or 1 cup fresh, diced tomatoes)
2 1/2 tablespoons fresh lime juice
1 teaspoon fresh lime zest
2 1/2 cups yellow split peas, sorted, rinsed, and drained or 2 cups red lentils
1 teaspoon ground cinnamon
Freshly ground black pepper, to taste

Instructions

Sauté the onions and mushrooms:
- Heat 1/2 cup of the vegetable broth (or water) over medium heat
- Add the onion and garlic and a pinch of the sea salt
- Cook and stir for 5 minutes, or until the onion has softened
- Add the mushrooms and another pinch of sea salt
- Cook and stir for 5 to 10 more minutes, or until the mushrooms have softened

Add the rest of the ingredients and cook the stew:
- Add the remaining vegetable broth (or water), tomato paste, fire-roasted tomatoes, lime juice, lime zest, yellow split peas (or red lentils), and cinnamon
- Stir to combine, cover and simmer on low for 90 minutes, or until the split peas (or lentils) are tender but not mushy
- Season with sea salt and black pepper

To serve:
- Serve hot alongside a platter of Persian rice

—

Side

PERSIAN RICE WITH CURRANTS

—

—

PERSIAN RICE WITH CURRANTS

Serves 8

Don't be intimidated when it comes to making Persian rice. With a little patience in following the proper steps, you will have delicious, fluffy steamed rice that everyone will enjoy!

Tools

Fine mesh strainer
Large saucepan
Cooking oil spray
Wooden spoon
2 paper towels
Medium bowl
Small glass bowl
Large serving platter

Optional:
Electric rice cooker

Ingredients

4 cups white basmati rice, rinsed and drained
8 cups water
1 1/2 teaspoons sea salt, or to taste
1/2 cup water
1/2 cup dried currants

For the rice garnish:
2 tablespoons water
1/2 teaspoon turmeric
1/4 cup chopped fresh dill, or more to taste

Instructions

Wash the rice:
- Using your hands, vigorously rinse the raw rice in a fine mesh strainer with cold water
- Repeat 3 to 5 times until the rice water rinses clear

Parboil the rice in a large saucepan:
- Put the 8 cups of water and sea salt in the pan
- Bring to a boil, covered, over medium-high heat
- Add the rice and cook for 7 minutes, on medium-high heat, stirring occasionally
- Turn off the heat and pour the rice into a fine mesh strainer to drain

Steam the rice:
- Wash the saucepan
- Spray lightly with cooking oil (or lightly spray a rice cooker with cooking oil)
- Place the drained rice in the saucepan (or rice cooker)
- Pour 1/2 cup of water over the rice
- Use the end of a wooden spoon to poke 5 or 6 holes throughout the rice to the bottom of the pot
- Put 2 paper towels on top of the rice
- Cover tightly with the saucepan lid
- Cook on low heat for 40 minutes
- Turn off the heat
- Add currants to the rice in the saucepan (or rice cooker) and mix gently

—

PERSIAN RICE WITH CURRANTS

Serves 8

(...continued)

Instructions

Make the garnish:

- Scoop out 2 cups of the rice and place aside in a medium mixing bowl to make the rice garnish

- Mix together the 2 tablespoons of water with the turmeric in a small glass bowl

- Add to the 2 cups of reserved rice (from above)

To serve:

- Scoop the rice out of the saucepan and transfer it to a serving platter

- Use this yellow garnish rice to decorate the top of the plated rice

- Top sparingly with chopped dill

———

Side

CUCUMBER SALAD WITH CREAMY DRESSING

—

—

CUCUMBER SALAD WITH CREAMY DRESSING

Serves 8

This cucumber salad with its creamy dressing is a
cooling accompaniment to the warm stew.

Tools

Blender or food processor
Large glass bowl
Colander

Ingredients

10 cups English cucumbers, peeled
(from about 2 1/2 cucumbers)
1 teaspoon sea salt (or more to taste)
1/3 cup diced red onion (from 1 small onion)
Freshly ground black pepper
1/4 cup chopped fresh mint or more
(or to taste)
1/4 cup chopped fresh parsley or more
(or to taste)

Creamy "Yogurt" Dressing:
1 1/2 cups of plain non-dairy yogurt
2 teaspoons brown sugar
2 teaspoons lemon juice
1/2 teaspoon sea salt, or to taste

Instructions

Prep the cucumbers and onion:
- Using the thinnest blade on the food processor,
  thinly slice the cucumbers

- Place the sliced cucumbers in a large glass bowl and
  add the sea salt and mix

- Place the red onion in the bowl and fold together with
  the cucumbers

Assemble the salad with the dressing:
- Add the creamy dressing (below), freshly ground
  black pepper to taste, mint, and parsley to the large bowl

- Mix to coat evenly

- Chill before serving

Make the dressing:
- Place all the ingredients in a blender or food
  processor, and blend until smooth

—

Dessert

HAMANTASCHEN COOKIES

—

—

jewishfoodhero.com

HAMANTASCHEN COOKIES

Makes approximately 30 cookies

These festive cookies are a traditional Purim food, and fun for
little ones to help make (always under adult supervision)!

Tools

Small bowl

Whisk

Medium mixing bowl

Large mixing bowl

Wooden spoon or electric mixer

Plastic wrap

Parchment paper

3-inch round cookie cutter or you can use
the rim of a glass

Spatula

Cooking oil

Baking sheet

Cooling rack

Small mesh strainer for sprinkling
powdered sugar

Ingredients

2 tablespoons arrowroot flour

3 tablespoons unsweetened low-fat non-dairy
milk (or water)

2 1/4 cups all-purpose flour OR gluten-free
baking mix (such as Bob's Red Mill Gluten
Free All Purpose Baking Flour)

1 teaspoon aluminum-free baking powder

1/4 teaspoon sea salt

1/2 cup virgin coconut oil, softened (check the
bottle to make sure it can be heated to 350 F)

1/2 cup organic cane sugar

1 teaspoon fresh orange zest

1/4 cup orange juice

1 teaspoon vanilla extract

1 jar all-fruit jam, in the flavor of your choice

Ingredients Continued

Optional cookie garnish:
1/4 cup powdered sugar

Instructions

• Preheat the oven to 350 F

In a small bowl:

• Combine the arrowroot flour and the milk.
  Mix well with a fork or small whisk until smooth.

Prepare the dry mixture:

• In a medium bowl, whisk together the flour,
  baking powder, and salt, and set aside

Prepare the wet mixture:

• In a large bowl, cream the coconut oil and sugar
  together with the orange zest. You can do so by hand or
  with an electric mixer.

• Add the arrowroot mixture and mix with a wooden
  spoon to combine

• Add the juice and extract, and mix until combined

Combine the two mixtures to form the dough:

• Add the dry mixture to the wet, and stir to combine.
  Be careful to not overmix.

• You can work with the dough right away or chill it in the
  refrigerator for 20 to 30 minutes (but no longer or it will
  get too firm)

———

jewishfoodhero.com

HAMANTASCHEN COOKIES

Makes approximately 30 cookies

(...continued)

Instructions

Meanwhile:
- Lightly oil a baking sheet

Form the cookies and bake:
- Roll out the dough between two sheets of parchment paper, to 1/8-inch thickness (you can do this in two batches if you wish)

- Lightly flour the parchment paper or dough if the dough is sticking

- Use a 3-inch round cookie cutter or the rim of a glass to cut circles from the rolled dough

- Using a spatula, carefully transfer the circles to the baking sheet

- Place a teaspoon of jam in the center of each circle

- Carefully form three sides with the dough and fold them over to create a triangle

- Pinch the corners tightly (like you mean it)

- Repeat with the remaining circles of dough

- Bake for 20 minutes, then remove from the oven

- Cool cookies on a cooling rack

Once completely cooled:
- Garnish with a sprinkling of powdered sugar if desired before serving

—

—

PESACH

—

—

PESACH

The Inspiration Behind This Menu

In my imagination, we're at a lush farm in the country preparing this meal together in the kitchen. We've picked ingredients from a vegetable garden for the meal. My skin feels warm from the sun, and I can hear the sounds of our families' laughter combined with the sounds of nature and animals.

To me, Pesachh is an invitation for food simplicity. It allows your body to experience true "freedom" during a special seven-day period. Keeping things simple allows you to focus on how you feel and the experiences you're creating (instead of worrying about a particular advanced cooking technique or dreading feeling stuffed after the meal).

This meal celebrates the spring season and fresh food. It's a simple meal that can be combined with spring colors on your table and requires minimal preparation. It's about fresh ingredients and easy recipes that leave you feeling nourished.

—

Energetic Theme: *Freedom*

MENU

—

DIP

Parsnip Tahini Spread

APPETIZER

Chilled Pink Cucumber Soup*

MAIN DISH

Vegetarian Shepherd's Pie

SIDE

Green Salad With Fresh Herbs

DESSERT

Pistachio Apple Cake

*This recipe can be prepared by children with adult supervision.

—

jewishfoodhero.com

Dip

PARSNIP TAHINI SPREAD

—

—

PARSNIP TAHINI SPREAD

Makes 4 cups

Enjoy this rich and creamy vegetable spread on your matzo for a delicious appetizer.
It tastes (and looks) beautiful garnished with sliced radishes, parsley, and grated beet.

Tools

Medium saucepan
Colander
Large bowl
Blender or food processor
Medium serving bowl
Serving plate for matzo

Ingredients

2 1/2 cups peeled and sliced parsnips
(from about 3 large parsnips)
3 teaspoons sliced scallions (white part only)
1/4 cup plus 2 tablespoons tahini
1 tablespoon plus 1 teaspoon kosher for
Passover white wine vinegar
2 teaspoons sea salt
White pepper to taste

Garnishing options:
Sliced red radishes
Chopped fresh parsley
Grated beet

Instructions

Cook the parsnips:
- Place the prepped parsnips in a medium saucepan and cover with 1 inch of water

- Boil for 20 minutes, or until fork-tender

- Drain the parsnips over a large bowl, and reserve the cooking water

- Place the cooked parsnips in a blender along with the remaining ingredients, and puree until smooth

- Add just enough reserved cooking water to achieve the desired consistency

Garnish and serve:
- Transfer the spread to a serving bowl, and garnish with the options of your choice

- Serve alongside a serving plate of matzo

—

CHILLED PINK CUCUMBER SOUP

—

—

CHILLED PINK CUCUMBER SOUP

Makes 8 cups

This cool and creamy cucumber soup is light and delicious.
It makes a striking appearance on the table with its lovely pink color.

Tools

Blender or food processor
Individual soup bowls for serving

Ingredients

2 cups raw unsalted cashews, soaked
overnight and drained
3 cups peeled, cored, and chopped red apples
(from about 4 medium apples)
4 1/2 cups peeled and chopped cucumbers
(from about 3 medium cucumbers)
2 cups almond milk
1/4 cup plus 2 tablespoons lemon juice
1 1/2 tablespoons chopped scallions
(white part only)
1 tablespoon sea salt, or more to taste
2 1/2 tablespoons grated raw beets
White pepper to taste

Garnishing options:
Fresh dill
Sliced radishes
Diced cucumber
Fresh mint

Instructions

In a blender or food processor:
- Place all the soup ingredients and blend until smooth

Garnish and serve:
- Serve chilled in individual soup bowls, garnished
  with your choice of garnishing options

—

Main Dish

VEGETARIAN SHEPHERD'S PIE

—

—

VEGETARIAN SHEPHERD'S PIE

Serves 8

This version of shepherd's pie celebrates vegetables in a light, springy version of a family favorite.

Tools

Extra large pot
Large skillet
Small bowl
Colander
Potato masher
Glass baking dish (9 x 13 inch)
Large spoon
Medium pot and steamer basket

Ingredients

Mashed potatoes topping:
3 pounds red skinned potatoes, peeled and cut into large chunks
1 cup almond milk
Pepper to taste
1 teaspoon sea salt

Pie filling:
2 cups diced onion (from about 2 medium onions)
3 cups sliced mushrooms
(from about 1/2 pound whole mushrooms)
3 cups vegetable broth (not low sodium)
1 teaspoon fresh sage, minced
2 tablespoons fresh thyme, minced
2 cups, peeled and sliced carrots
(from about 2 carrots)
2 cups cauliflower florets
(from about 1 small head)
3 tablespoons potato starch
1 teaspoon sea salt
Pepper to taste

Instructions

- Preheat the oven to 350 F

Boil the potatoes:
- Place the prepared potatoes in an extra large soup pot, and cover with at least 1 inch of cold water
- Boil, uncovered, for 20 minutes, or until the potatoes are fork-tender

Meanwhile, sauté the vegetables:
- In a large skillet, sauté the onion and mushrooms in 1/4 cup vegetable broth or water for 10 minutes, adding more broth if needed
- Add the sage, thyme, and carrots, and sauté for another 5 minutes
- Add the cauliflower and cook for 5 more minutes
- Add the vegetable broth to the vegetables in the skillet, reserving 1/4 cup to mix with potato starch

Create the potato starch slurry and finish cooking the vegetable mixture:
- In a small bowl, combine the potato starch with the 1/4 cup reserved vegetable broth. Mix well.
- Add the potato starch mixture, sea salt, and pepper to the vegetables
- Stir until thickened

Mash the potatoes:
- Drain the cooked potatoes and mash them, adding the almond milk, pepper, and sea salt

---

VEGETARIAN SHEPHERD'S PIE

Serves 8

(...continued)

Ingredients

Topping:

Steamed carrots, yellow summer squash, and zucchini (cut into rounds)*

If you eat kitniyot during Passover, you can also use peas and thin string beans here.

Instructions

Assemble the dish and bake:

- Pour the cooked vegetables into a lightly oiled 9 x 13-inch glass casserole dish

- Top with the mashed potatoes and smooth the surface with a spoon

- Bake for 30 minutes

Prepare the garnish:

- While the casserole is cooking, chop the vegetables for the garnish, paying attention to maintaining a uniform and delicate shape

- Steam the vegetables for the garnish just enough so they retain their beautiful color and a bit of crunch

Arrange the garnish and serve:

- Arrange the warm vegetables on top of the casserole in a design that inspires you

- Keep warm in the oven until ready to serve. Serve family style on the table.

—

Side

GREEN SALAD WITH FRESH HERBS

—

—

jewishfoodhero.com

GREEN SALAD WITH FRESH HERBS

Serves 8

This lovely green salad is a flavorful combination of fresh herbs and spring greens, complemented with a simple sweet lime dressing.

Instructions

In a large bowl:

- Place all the prepped salad ingredients

Make the dressing and assemble the salad:

- Place all the salad dressing ingredients in a salad dressing shaker bottle

- Shake well and pour as much as you wish over the salad, just before serving

- Toss lightly to coat evenly

To serve:

- Serve family style on the table

Tools

Large salad bowl
Salad dressing shaker bottle

Ingredients

4 heads lettuce
(butter crunch and/or green leaf)
2 cups scallions
(just the green tops) (from about 2 bunches)
1 bunch fresh mint, de-stemmed and chopped
1 bunch fresh cilantro, de-stemmed
and chopped

Simple lime dressing:
1/2 cup liquid sugar cane syrup
1/2 cup lime juice (from about 4 small limes)
1 teaspoon sea salt, or more to taste
2 teaspoons minced shallots or garlic
(from about 2 small shallots or 4 garlic cloves)

PISTACHIO APPLE CAKE

—

—

PISTACHIO APPLE CAKE

Serves 8

Moist, flavorful, and satisfying without being heavy, this apple cake
will make the perfect dessert to complete your Pesachh menu.

Tools

Medium mixing bowl

Large mixing bowl

Grater

2 small bowls

Cooking oil

8-inch cake pan or springform pan

Ingredients

Cake:

3/4 cup matzo meal (or matzo cake meal)

1/4 cup potato starch

1 teaspoon kosher for Passover baking
powder

1/2 teaspoon sea salt

1/2 cup applesauce

1/2 cup finely grated yellow summer squash
(from about 1 small summer squash)

1 cup sugar

1/4 cup orange juice

1 flax "egg": 1 tablespoon ground flax seeds
mixed with 3 tablespoons water

Instructions

- Preheat the oven to 350 F

Make the cake batter:

Prepare the dry ingredients:
- In a medium bowl, whisk together the matzo meal,
  potato starch, baking powder, and salt, and set aside

Prepare the wet ingredients:
- In a large bowl, combine the applesauce, summer
  squash, sugar, orange juice, flax "egg," and water

- Stir to combine and set aside

Combine the two mixtures:
- Add the dry mixture to the wet, and stir to combine
  until you have a smooth batter

Make the cinnamon sugar mixture:
- In a small bowl, mix together the cinnamon, nutmeg,
  and sugar

Assemble the cake and bake:
- Pour half the cake batter into a lightly oiled cake pan
  or springform pan

- Top with half the prepared apple slices

- Sprinkle with half the cinnamon sugar mixture

- Spread the remaining cake batter on top

- Arrange the remaining apple slices in a pretty pattern
  on top of the cake

- Sprinkle with the remaining cinnamon sugar mixture
  and the chopped pistachios

- Bake for 40 minutes

—

jewishfoodhero.com

PISTACHIO APPLE CAKE

Serves 8

(...continued)

Instructions

To serve:

- Serve warm or cool
- Serve either as is, or with a scoop of non-dairy vanilla ice cream (if serving hot), or with a sprinkling of kosher for Passover powdered sugar if serving cool

Ingredients

Apple filling:
3 large Granny Smith apples, peeled, cored, and thinly sliced

Cinnamon sugar:
1 teaspoon ground cinnamon
1/4 teaspoon ground nutmeg
1/2 cup sugar

Topping:
2–3 tablespoons chopped unsalted pistachios

Optional garnish:
Non-dairy vanilla ice cream (if planning to serve hot) or a sprinkling of kosher for Passover powdered sugar (if planning to serve cool)

LAG B'OMER

—

www.jewishfoodhero.com

—

LAG B'OMER

The Inspiration Behind This Menu

When I was seeking inspiration for this menu, I had only two things on my mind—cooking outside and bonfires.

When one of my friends wrote a Facebook post about how much she missed Texas barbecue, it brought me back to my 20s when I lived and worked in Austin. Since I was vegan at the time, I was pretty much only eating the barbecue sides of cornbread, pickles, and coleslaw. Even so, I still enjoyed the barbecue atmosphere and the community surrounding this eating ritual.

I created this menu imagining that I was back in Texas, and spending time in a backyard with friends, a roaring bonfire, and a healthy barbecue meal at last.

—

MENU

—

APPETIZER

Blueberry Apple Smoothie

MAIN DISH

Black Bean Bites
With Barbecue Sauce

SIDE

Green Bean and New Potato Salad

SIDE

Nutritious Cornbread*

DESSERT

Maple-Peach Oat Crumble

*This recipe can be prepared by children with adult supervision.

—

Appetizer

BLUEBERRY APPLE SMOOTHIE

—

—

jewishfoodhero.com

BLUEBERRY APPLE SMOOTHIE

Serves 8

This is a very refreshing start to a Lag B'Omer barbecue that is otherwise filled with so many smoky and savory notes. Feel free to vary the fruit based on what is in season near you.

Instructions

In a blender:

- Place all the prepped ingredients and puree until smooth

- Serve in small glasses or shooters

Tools

Blender
Small serving glasses or shooters

Ingredients

2 1/2 cups fresh or frozen blueberries
2 cups peeled and chopped cucumbers
(from about 2 small cucumbers)
2 1/2 cups apple juice
2 cups ice

Optional:
2 tablespoons fresh mint

Main Dish

BLACK BEAN BITES WITH BARBECUE SAUCE

—

—

BLACK BEAN BITES WITH BARBECUE SAUCE

Serves 8 (32 mini bites)

These hearty little black bean bites combine whole-grain brown rice, black beans, and sweet potato to make a satisfying mini burger. Make this recipe into small patty bites for a pretty presentation.

Tools

Medium skillet
Colander
Large bowl
Potato masher or fork
Box grater
Parchment paper
Baking sheet
Cooking oil spray
Spatula
Large serving platter

Ingredients

1/4 cup vegetable broth (or water)
1/2 cup diced red onion (from 1/2 onion)
1 teaspoon sea salt, or to taste
4 cups cooked black beans
(about two 15-ounce cans, drained well [or from 1 1/3 cups dry beans, soaked, and boiled until tender])
3 cups peeled and grated sweet potatoes
(from about 4 medium sweet potatoes)
1 1/2 cups cooked brown rice
(from 1/3 cup raw rice)
1/4 cup ketchup
2 tablespoons minced cilantro
1/2 cup finely sliced scallions
2 teaspoons ground cumin
1/2 cup unbleached white flour
(or gluten-free all-purpose flour)
Whole leaves from 1 head romaine lettuce, for serving

Instructions

• Preheat the oven to 350 F

Sauté the onion:

• Heat a medium skillet over medium heat

• Add the vegetable broth, red onion, and a pinch of the sea salt

• Cook and stir for 5 to 10 minutes, or until the onion is soft

If you are using canned beans:

• Place the cooked black beans in a colander and rinse multiple times

Form the patties:

• Place the cooked black beans in a large bowl

• Mash partially with a potato masher

• Stir in the remaining ingredients

• If the mixture seems too dry, add a small amount of water

• If the mixture seems too wet, add a little more flour

• Form into small patties (with wet hands)

——

BLACK BEAN BITES WITH BARBECUE SAUCE

Serves 8 (32 mini bites)

(...continued)

Instructions

Bake or grill the patties:
If grilling, do <u>not</u> use parchment paper and spray. Simply lightly grease your grill and grill as you would any other burger.

- Place a piece of parchment paper flat on your baking sheet

- Spray the parchment paper lightly with cooking oil spray (this is important, so the patties do not stick to the paper)

- Place the patties onto the parchment paper

- Bake for 15 minutes, then flip the patties and bake for another 15 minutes on the second side

- Cool for 15 minutes to let them firm up a bit before serving

- Feel free to grill them on a preheated grill for a few minutes on each side to add a nice flavor

To serve:
- Serve on a large serving platter in individual lettuce leaves, with a dollop of barbecue sauce (recipe on the next page)

—

HOMEMADE BARBECUE SAUCE

Makes 2 cups

Top off your black bean bites with this robust barbecue sauce.
Consider making a double batch!

Instructions

In a small saucepan:

- Heat all the ingredients together on low heat, covered, for 15 minutes

- Whisk frequently, making sure that it does not stick to the saucepan

- Pour into a medium serving bowl, and refrigerate before serving

Tools

Small saucepan
Whisk
Medium serving bowl

Ingredients

1 1/2 cups ketchup
1 1/2 teaspoons onion powder
1 tablespoon apple cider vinegar
2 tablespoons mustard
2 tablespoons maple syrup

Optional:
1 tablespoon vegan Worcestershire sauce

---

jewishfoodhero.com

GREEN BEAN AND NEW POTATO SALAD

—

—

GREEN BEAN AND NEW POTATO SALAD

Serves 8

This is a lighter take on traditional potato salad and is filling, fresh, and full of flavor.
This salad perfectly combines steamed potatoes and crisp fresh green beans,
and will add a beautiful bright appearance to your plate.

Tools

Large cooking pot with steamer basket
Large bowl
Medium bowl with ice water
Large mesh strainer
Serving bowl
Rubber spatula
Small bowl
Whisk

Ingredients

6 cups new potatoes (cut into bite-size pieces)
1/2 teaspoon sea salt
4 cups trimmed fresh green beans, cut into
2-inch lengths
1/4 cup diced red onion (or scallions),
or more to taste

Instructions

Steam the potatoes:

- Place the washed new potatoes in a steamer basket over a large pot filled with 1 inch of cold water

- Sprinkle the potatoes with the sea salt

- Bring the water to a boil over medium-high heat

- Cover and reduce the heat to simmer on medium low for 12 minutes or until the potatoes are fork-tender

- Carefully remove the potatoes from the steamer basket and place them in a large bowl

- Set aside to let cool slightly, then place in the refrigerator to chill while assembling the green beans

Steam the green beans:

- Place the washed and cut green beans in the same steamer basket

- Steam the green beans just until they are bright green and tender, approximately 10 minutes (Pay attention not to overcook the green beans so as to preserve their color and a bit of crunch. This will prevent the salad from taking on a mushy unattractive quality.)

- Carefully remove the green beans from the steamer basket, and transfer them to a medium bowl filled with ice water. This will shock the beans and stop the cooking process.

- Once cooled, strain the ice water using a large fine mesh strainer, and set aside

—

GREEN BEAN AND NEW POTATO SALAD

Serves 8

(...continued)

Instructions

Assemble the salad:

- In a large bowl, combine the potatoes and green beans, and top with the red onion or scallions

- Add the dressing (below) and gently fold to combine using a rubber spatula (take care not to crush the ingredients as you fold)

Make the dressing:

- In a small bowl, whisk together all the dressing ingredients

- Pour over the assembled Green Bean and New Potato Salad

- Adjust seasoning to taste

Ingredients

Smokey-Sweet Dressing:
1/2 cup red wine vinegar
(or any other vinegar of your choice)
1/4 cup grainy mustard
3 teaspoons smoked salt or sea salt
Freshly ground black pepper to taste
2 tablespoons sugar
3 tablespoons fresh minced dill
(or 3 teaspoons dried dill)

Optional:
3 teaspoons vegan Worcestershire sauce
2 tablespoons minced fresh parsley

NUTRITIOUS CORNBREAD

—

—

NUTRITIOUS CORNBREAD

Serves 8 (makes 16 small squares)

Nothing rounds out a barbecue like cornbread (it's practically a requirement). Serve the cornbread cut into small squares for easy eating.

Tools

Large mixing bowl
Whisk
Medium bowl
Cooking oil
8-inch square baking pan
Toothpick
Platter for serving

Ingredients

Dry ingredients:
1 cup cornmeal
1 cup unbleached white flour or gluten-free all-purpose flour
2 teaspoons baking powder
1/2 teaspoon sea salt

Wet ingredients:
1 cup rice milk (or water)
1/2 cup applesauce
1/4 cup maple syrup

Instructions

- Preheat the oven to 350 F

Prepare the dry mixture:
- Place all of the dry ingredients in a large bowl and whisk together

Prepare the wet mixture:
- Place all of the wet ingredients in a medium bowl and whisk together

- Add the wet ingredients to the dry ingredients

- Mix just until all the ingredients are evenly moist, and then stop

Prepare the pan, and bake the cornbread:
- Lightly oil an 8-inch square baking pan, and pour the batter into it

- Bake for 40 minutes, or until a toothpick comes out clean when inserted in the center

- Cool completely before cutting into small squares and arranging on a platter

- Serve with the spread of your choice

—

Dessert

MAPLE-PEACH OAT CRUMBLE

—

—

MAPLE-PEACH OAT CRUMBLE

Serves 8

This is a healthy and yummy version of a traditional peach cobbler.
Make two if you want to have an extra one for a special breakfast the next day.

Tools

Small bowl
Large bowl
Medium bowl
Cooking oil
9-inch pie plate
(a glass pie plate if you want to be fancy)
Small individual serving bowls

Ingredients

Maple peach filling:
1 tablespoon cornstarch
8 cups diced, peeled fresh or frozen peaches
(from about 12 medium peaches)
1/4 teaspoon sea salt
1/2 teaspoon ground cinnamon
1 1/2 teaspoons fresh lemon juice
1/4 cup brown sugar or maple syrup
1/4 cup plus 2 tablespoons all-purpose flour
or gluten-free all-purpose flour

Sweet oat crumble:
3/4 cup quick oats
3/4 cup unbleached flour or gluten-free all-
purpose flour
3/4 cup brown sugar
2 tablespoons apple juice
1 1/2 teaspoons vanilla extract
1/2 teaspoon sea salt

Garnish:
Non-dairy fruit sorbet or non-dairy vanilla
ice cream

Instructions

- Preheat the oven to 350 F

Create the cornstarch slurry:
- Place 1 tablespoon cornstarch in a small bowl

- Add 1 tablespoon of cold water to the cornstarch,
  and mix well until smooth

Prepare the maple peach filling:
- Place all the ingredients together in a large bowl,
  and stir to coat evenly

Prepare the sweet oat crumble:
- Combine the oats, flour, and sugar in a medium bowl

- Add the rest of the wet ingredients, and mix to combine

Assemble the crumble:
- Lightly oil a 9-inch pie plate

- Place peaches evenly in the pie plate

- Spread the sweet oat crumble evenly over the peaches

- Bake for 30 to 40 minutes, or until golden brown on
  top and bubbly

- Serve hot

Garnish and serve:
- Scoop the crumble into small individual serving
  bowls, and garnish with 1 scoop of non-dairy fruit
  sorbet or non-dairy ice cream

—

SHAVUOT

—

—

SHAVUOT

The Inspiration Behind This Menu

One of the traditions associated with Shavuot is the consumption of dairy products like milk and cheese. I wanted to participate in the Shavuot meal festivities while updating this tradition to include more healthful dairy substitutes. So I created a delicious and creamy meal for those who are sensitive to dairy, or who live a vegan or plant-based lifestyle.

As a backdrop, I imagined that this menu could be served in a non-dairy Jewish diner in New York City (can you imagine!).

This menu is also special because I tested it out for my mother's birthday in August 2014. My brothers, father, and I, with our respective spouses, organized a dinner for my Mom at a local cafe in a tiny sleepy summer town in Maine.

I was in charge of the menu, and unbeknownst to everyone, requested that the cafe cook this entire Shavuot menu and serve it family style for the birthday dinner. Everyone loved it, and I felt really happy to share the menu with my family and to have them enjoying such healthy food.

Now you can enjoy it too!

—

Energetic Theme: *Devotion*

MENU

—

APPETIZER

Pink Gazpacho*

MAIN DISH

Creamy Baked Pasta
With Bread Crumb Topping

SIDE

Joni's 24-Hour Cucumber Salad

SIDE

Rainbow Quinoa Salad

DESSERT

Lemon "Cheesecake"

*This recipe can be prepared by children with adult supervision.

—

jewishfoodhero.com

Appetizer

PINK GAZPACHO

—

—

PINK GAZPACHO

Serves 8

This fruity version of gazpacho can be made sweet or savory, depending on your taste.
The lovely ruby color is offset nicely when garnished with mint sprigs.

Tools

Blender or food processor
Shooters or individual small bowls for serving

Ingredients

9 cups cubed seeded watermelon
(from about one 3-pound melon)
2 cups peeled, chopped English cucumbers
1 1/4 cups apple juice
3 teaspoons lemon juice
6 fresh mint leaves, minced
1/2 teaspoon sea salt

Optional additions:
Honey, diced onion, minced jalapeño, red bell
pepper, black pepper, to taste

Garnish:
Mint sprigs

Instructions

In a blender or food processor:
- Puree all the ingredients until the desired consistency—you can make it smooth or leave a little texture as you wish

- Taste and adjust seasoning

To serve:
- Serve in shooters or individual small bowls

—

Main Dish

CREAMY BAKED PASTA WITH BREAD CRUMB TOPPING

—

—

CREAMY BAKED PASTA WITH BREAD CRUMB TOPPING

Serves 8

This baked pasta dish is made with mushrooms, onions, and a creamy sauce,
and is topped off with a layer of crunchy bread crumbs.

Tools

Aluminum foil

Baking sheet

Medium stockpot

Colander to drain cooked pasta

Skillet

Small bowl

Large bowl

Cooking oil

Glass baking dish (9 x 13 inch)

Spatula

Ingredients

8 cloves garlic, roasted
(add up to 12 cloves if you love garlic)

4 shallots, roasted (add up to 6 shallots)

4 cups uncooked elbow or penne pasta
(can use gluten-free)

1/2 cup vegetable broth (or water)

2 cups thinly sliced onion (from 2 onions)

1 teaspoon sea salt, or to taste

24 ounces button mushrooms, thinly sliced

4 cups unsweetened, low-fat non-dairy milk

6 tablespoons nutritional yeast

1 teaspoon onion powder

1/2 teaspoon garlic powder

3 teaspoons prepared mustard

1/2 teaspoon ground nutmeg

1/2 teaspoon turmeric powder

1/2 cup unbleached flour(or cornstarch or
arrowroot powder for gluten-free)

1/2 cup cold water

1/2 cup breadcrumbs (can use gluten-free)

Instructions

• Preheat the oven to 400 F

Roast the garlic and shallots:
• Slice the top off a bulb of garlic

• Wrap in aluminum foil

• Repeat with the shallots

• Place both on a baking sheet and bake for 35 to 45
minutes, until soft inside, making sure they do
not burn

• Once this is done, turn the oven down to 350 F

Meanwhile, cook the pasta:
• Fill the stockpot with at least 8 cups of water

• Cook the pasta very *al dente* (as you will be baking
it later)

• Drain in a colander and rinse with cool water.
Set aside.

While the pasta is cooking, sauté the vegetables:
• In a skillet, heat the vegetable broth (or water)
over medium-high heat

• Add the prepped onions and a pinch of the sea salt

• Cook and stir for 5 minutes or until the onions are soft

• Add the mushrooms and another pinch of sea salt

• Cook and stir for 5 more minutes, or until the
mushrooms are tender

• Add the non-dairy milk, roasted garlic and shallots,
nutritional yeast, sea salt, onion powder, garlic powder,
mustard, nutmeg, and turmeric powder to the onion-
mushroom mixture and stir gently

———

CREAMY BAKED PASTA WITH BREAD CRUMB TOPPING

Serves 8

(...continued)

Instructions

Make a cornstarch slurry and add to the vegetables to thicken:

- In a small bowl, combine the cornstarch with the cold water and stir well to combine

- Add the cornstarch to the onion-mushroom mixture and stir for a few minutes over medium heat until thickened

- Add more diluted cornstarch if needed to achieve the desired consistency

Combine the noodles and the vegetable mixture:

- In a large bowl, combine the cooked pasta with the onion and mushroom mixture

- Make sure the pasta is evenly covered

Prepare the baking dish, and topping, and bake:

- Lightly oil the baking dish

- Transfer the pasta into the dish

- Smooth the top with a spatula and sprinkle evenly with the breadcrumbs

- Cover with foil and bake for 30 minutes

- Remove the foil and bake for an additional 10 minutes, until the top is lightly browned

To serve:

- Let cool slightly and serve family style on the table

———

Side

JONI'S 24-HOUR CUCUMBER SALAD

—

—

jewishfoodhero.com

JONI'S 24-HOUR CUCUMBER SALAD

Serves 8

This salad is light, refreshing, and easy to prepare in advance! For best results,
let the salted cucumbers "sleep" overnight as they drain.

Instructions

Prep the cucumbers:

- Peel and thinly slice the cucumbers (ideally with a food processor using the thinnest slice blade). If you don't have a food processor, make sure the slices are very thin.

- Place the cucumbers in a large glass bowl

- Add the sea salt and rub it into the cucumbers

- Place a small plate directly on top of the cucumbers, then add a very heavy object on top to squeeze the waterout of the cucumbers (such as a large stone or large water bottles)

- Let the cucumbers rest like this overnight, or at least 6 hours

- Drain off the excess water occasionally

- When complete, place the cucumbers in a colander and rinse

- Press the excess moisture out of the cucumbers with a kitchen towel

- Transfer the cucumbers to a serving bowl

- Optional: Mix onions into the cucumber salad

- Dress with the Sunshine Dressing (see the recipe on the next page)

Tools

Food processor with slicing blade
Large glass bowl
Small plate
Colander
Kitchen towel
Serving bowl

Ingredients

6 large English cucumbers
(peeled or unpeeled)
1 1/2 tablespoons sea salt

Optional:
1 cup diced red onion (from 1 medium onion)

———

SUNSHINE DRESSING

Instructions

In a medium bowl:

- Place all of the dressing ingredients, and whisk to combine

To serve:

- Pour the dressing over the cucumbers and toss to coat evenly

- Serve immediately in the bowl it was mixed in, or chill before serving

- This salad is best eaten the day it is dressed

Tools

Medium bowl
Whisk

Ingredients

1/2 cup fresh orange juice
1/4 cup fresh lemon juice
1/4 cup grainy mustard
Freshly ground black pepper to taste
2 tablespoons raw sugar or maple syrup

Optional:
1/4 cup minced fresh dill

RAINBOW QUINOA SALAD

—

—

RAINBOW QUINOA SALAD

Serves 8

Quinoa is high in protein and contains many essential amino acids. It has a sweet and
nutty flavor that can be very appealing. The quinoa and vegetables covered with
a lovely dressing make a colorful, light, and fresh-tasting side dish.

Tools

Mesh strainer
Medium saucepan
Fork
Large mixing bowl
Small bowl
Whisk

Ingredients

5 cups cooked quinoa
(from 1 cup plus 3 tablespoons raw quinoa)
4 cups low-sodium vegetable broth or water
(for cooking the quinoa)
1 1/2 cups sliced scallions
(from 2 small bunches)
1 1/2 cups grated carrots
(from about 5 medium carrots)
1 1/2 cups shredded red cabbage
(from about 1/4 medium head of cabbage)
1 1/2 cups minced parsley
(from 1 large bunch)

Optional:
1 clove garlic

Dressing:
1/2 cup orange juice
1/4 cup lemon juice
1 1/2 teaspoons sea salt, or to taste
Black pepper, to taste

Instructions

Prep and cook the quinoa:
- Rinse 2 cups of the dry quinoa in a mesh strainer

- Toast the quinoa in a medium saucepan over
  medium heat, stirring it for about 1 minute until the
  water evaporates and the quinoa is slightly toasted

- Add 4 cups of the low-sodium vegetable broth

- Bring to a boil and then place on medium heat and
  cover and cook for approximately 20 minutes

- When completely cooked, turn off the heat and leave
  covered for 5 minutes

- After 5 minutes, fluff the quinoa with a fork

Prepare the vegetables and then assemble the salad:
- Place the scallions, carrots, red cabbage,
  and parsley in a large bowl

- Fold the quinoa into the salad mixture

Prepare the dressing and pour over the salad:
- In a separate small bowl, whisk together all of the
  dressing ingredients

- Pour over the quinoa and vegetables and mix gently
  with your hands to evenly coat

To serve:
- Serve chilled or at room temperature, in the bowl it
  was mixed in, family style on the table

—

jewishfoodhero.com

Dessert

LEMON "CHEESECAKE"

—

—

LEMON "CHEESECAKE"

Serves 8 (makes one 8-inch cheesecake)

This is a yummy, lower-fat, plant-based version of cheesecake.
With the addition of lemon, it tastes light and is the perfect summer dessert.

Tools

Food processor
Cooking oil
Springform cheesecake pan (8 inch)
Offset spatula
Dessert platter for serving

Ingredients

Crust:
2 cups graham cracker crumbs
1/4 cup chopped dates
1/4 teaspoon sea salt

Cheesecake:
28 ounces silken tofu, drained
1/4 cup lemon juice
1/2 teaspoon sea salt
2 cups sugar
2 teaspoons vanilla
1/2 teaspoon sea salt
2 tablespoons tahini

Garnish:
Lemon twists and fresh berries

Instructions

• Preheat the oven to 350 F

Make the crust:

• Place the graham cracker crumbs, dates, and sea salt in a food processor

• Blend until crumbly (it should stick together when pressed with your fingers)

• Transfer to a lightly oiled springform pan and press evenly onto the bottom to form a crust

• Rinse and dry the food processor, and set aside

Make the cheesecake batter:

• Place all the cheesecake batter ingredients in the food processor and blend until smooth

• Pour the batter over the crust and smooth the top with an offset spatula

• Bake for 30 minutes, or until set in the middle

• Remove from the oven and cool completely before removing from the springform pan, and place on a decorative dessert platter

Chill and serve:

• Once cooled, refrigerate for up to 4 hours to chill

• Garnish with lemon twists and fresh berries, and serve

ROSH HASHANAH

—

Sweet Squash Spread With Fresh Apple Slices

VEGETABLES
Butternut squash, 1 medium
Green onion, for garnish

HERBS
Fresh cilantro, for garnish

FRUITS
Gala or McIntosh apples, 3 medium, and 1 large for the side dish
Lemon, 1 for juicing

SPICES AND CONDIMENTS
Cumin, 1/2 teaspoon
Cinnamon, 1 teaspoon
Salt, to taste
Pepper, to taste

DRY INGREDIENTS
Optional: Challah or a round-shaped artisan bread

TOOLS
Large saucepan
Large bowl
Colander
Potato masher (or strong fork)
2 medium serving bowls
Small serving plate, for the apple slices
Medium serving plate, for the challah, if using

Ras El Hanout Vegetables Over Couscous

VEGETABLES
Zucchini, 3 medium
Turnips, 2 medium
Carrots, 4 large
Eggplants, 2 medium (2.5 pounds)
Onion, 1 large
Red bell peppers, 2

HERBS
Fresh mint, for garnish

FRUITS
Oranges, 3 for juicing

WET INGREDIENTS
Vegetable broth, 6 1/2 cups total

DRY INGREDIENTS
Instant couscous, 4 cups

SPICES AND CONDIMENTS
Ground cloves, 1/4 teaspoon
Allspice, 1 teaspoon (or 1/3 teaspoon each of cinnamon, cloves, and nutmeg)
Ground cumin, 1/2 teaspoon
Ground ginger, 1 teaspoon
Turmeric, 1/2 teaspoon
Black pepper, 1/4 teaspoon
Cardamom, 2 teaspoons
Cinnamon, 1 teaspoon
Coriander, 1 teaspoon
Nutmeg, 1/2 teaspoon
Optional: Cayenne pepper, 1/4 teaspoon
Salt, 1 teaspoon, or to taste

TOOLS
Large bowl
Small bowl
Orange juicer (manual or electric)
Blender
Rectangular baking dish (13 inch)
Aluminum foil
Steamer basket
Large serving bowl
Large saucepan with lid
Fork
Large serving platter
Small serving bowl for garnish

Citrus Carrot Salad

VEGETABLES
Carrots, 10 medium
Optional: Shallots, to taste
Optional: Green onion, to taste

HERBS
Parsley, 1 small bunch

FRUITS
Lemon, 2
Dried apricots, 1 cup chopped
Oranges, 3 for zesting and juicing

SPICES AND CONDIMENTS
Ground cumin, 2 teaspoons
Ground cinnamon, 2 teaspoons
Salt, to taste
Pepper, to taste

TOOLS
Small skillet
Food processor with coarse grater attachment or hand grater
Large salad bowl
Small bowl
Whisk

Garbanzo Beans in Red Sauce

VEGETABLES

Tomatoes, 12 medium (or fat-free organic tomato sauce, 4 cups)
Garlic, 3 cloves
Onion, 1
Green onion, for garnish

HERBS

Fresh cilantro, for garnish

FRUITS

Lemon, 1 for 1 tablespoon juice

WET INGREDIENTS

Garbanzo beans, 3 cups (from two 15-ounce cans)
Vegetable broth or water, 1/4 cup
Tomato paste, 2 tablespoons

SPICES AND CONDIMENTS

Cumin, 1 teaspoon
Cinnamon, 1/2 teaspoon
Salt, 1/2 teaspoon
Pepper, 1/4 teaspoon

TOOLS

Large pot, if using fresh beans
Colander
Blender or food processor, if using fresh tomatoes
Large saucepan
Medium serving bowl

Spiced Stuffed Apples

FRUITS

Gala apples (or any baking apple), 8 medium
Currants, 1/4 cup

WET INGREDIENTS

Peanut butter or almond butter, 2 1/2 tablespoons
Maple syrup, 2 1/2 tablespoons
Apple juice, 1/2 cup
Optional: Non-dairy vanilla ice cream

SPICES AND CONDIMENTS

Ground cardamom, 2 teaspoons
Ground cloves, 1 teaspoon
Ground cinnamon, 2 teaspoons plus more for garnish

TOOLS

Apple corer
Small bowl
Large skillet with lid
Serving dish

—

YOM KIPPUR

—

.jewishfoodhero.com

Creamy Lemon Pasta

HERBS
Fresh parsley, for garnish

FRUITS
Lemon, 2 for juicing

WET INGREDIENTS
Vegetable broth, 3 cups
Silken tofu, 3/4 cup

DRY INGREDIENTS
Unbleached flour (or gluten-free all-purpose flour), 1 tablespoon plus 1 teaspoon
Whole-wheat linguini, or gluten-free pasta of your choice, 1 1/2 pounds

SPICES AND CONDIMENTS
Turmeric, 1/2 teaspoon
Salt, 1 tablespoon plus 1 teaspoon, or to taste

TOOLS
Blender or food processor
Medium saucepan
Whisk
Large pot
Colander
Large serving bowl

Pesto White Bean Salad

VEGETABLES
Red onion, 1
Celery, 2 stalks
Carrots, 3 medium
Artichoke hearts packed in water, 1/2 cup

HERBS
Fresh sage leaves, 8

FRUITS
Optional: Pitted black olives, 1/2 cup quartered

WET INGREDIENTS
Red wine vinegar, 1/2 cup
Fava beans or cannellini beans, 3 cups (from two 15-ounce cans)

TOOLS
Small glass bowl
Colander
Large serving bowl

Pesto Dressing

VEGETABLES
Garlic, 1 clove

HERBS
Fresh basil, 1 cup

FRUITS
Lemon, 1 for 1 tablespoon juice

WET INGREDIENTS
Honey, 1 tablespoon

DRY INGREDIENTS
Pine nuts, 1 tablespoon

SPICES AND CONDIMENTS
Mustard, 1 tablespoon
Salt, to taste

TOOLS
Blender or food processor

Cardamom Coffee Cake

FRUITS
Lemon, 1 for 1–2 teaspoons juice

WET INGREDIENTS
Coconut oil, 1 teaspoon
Silken tofu, 1 cup
Applesauce, 1 cup
Avocado oil, 2 tablespoons
All-natural vanilla extract, 1 teaspoon
Almond extract, 1/2 teaspoon

DRY INGREDIENTS
Unbleached, all-purpose flour, or gluten-free all-purpose flour, 1 cup
Whole-wheat pastry flour, or gluten-free all-purpose flour, 1 cup
Baking soda, 1 teaspoon
Baking powder, 1 teaspoon
Sugar, 1 cup
Black currants, 3/4 cup

SPICES AND CONDIMENTS
Salt, 1/4 teaspoon
Ground cardamom, 1/2 teaspoon

Sugar-nut filling:
DRY INGREDIENTS
Chopped pecans, 1/2 cup
Sugar, or alternative sugar blend such as Madhava Better Baking Blend, 1/2 cup
Powdered sugar, for garnish

SPICES AND CONDIMENTS
Cinnamon, 1 1/2 teaspoons
Cardamom, 1/2 teaspoon

TOOLS

- Large mixing bowl
- Whisk
- High-powered blender or food processor
- Small bowl
- Cooking oil
- 1–2 mini Bundt pans
- Small mesh strainer for the powdered sugar garnish

White Bean Vegetable Soup

VEGETABLES

- Onions, 2 medium
- Garlic, 2 cloves
- Carrots, 3 medium
- Celery, 2 stalks
- Tomatoes, 2 medium
- Kale, 1 bunch

HERBS

- Fresh parsley, minced, for garnish

WET INGREDIENTS

- Low-sodium vegetable broth, 8 1/2 cups
- Cooked cannellini beans, 3 cups (from two 15-ounce cans, drained and rinsed)

DRY INGREDIENTS

- Whole-grain bread, 4 pieces

SPICES AND CONDIMENTS

- Salt, to taste
- Pepper, to taste

TOOLS

- Large soup pot
- Individual soup bowls

Butternut Risotto

VEGETABLES

- Onions, 2 medium
- Butternut squash, 1
- Sugar snap peas, for garnish

FRUITS

- Dried apricots, 1–3, for garnish
- Pomegranate seeds, 1 cup, for garnish

WET INGREDIENTS

- Low-sodium vegetable broth, 12 cups
- Water, 2 tablespoons
- White cooking wine, 2 cups

DRY INGREDIENTS

- Arborio rice (do not rinse), 4 cups

TOOLS

- 2 small bowls for garnishes
- Medium saucepan
- Large saucepan
- Soup ladle
- Wooden spoon
- Medium pot and steamer basket
- Medium bowl
- Large serving bowl
- Individual bowls for serving

SUKKOT

—

jewishfoodhero.com

Mushroom Soup With Tofu Cream

VEGETABLES
- Onions, 2 medium
- Sliced button mushrooms, 12 cups

HERBS
- Fresh dill, 1 small bunch (if not using dried)
- Fresh parsley, 1 bunch, for garnish

WET INGREDIENTS
- Low-sodium vegetable broth, 5 1/2 cups
- Soy sauce (or gluten-free tamari), 3 tablespoons
- Rice milk, 2 cups
- Strained tomatoes, 1/2 cup
- Tofu "sour cream" (below), for garnish

DRY INGREDIENTS
- Optional: Flour, 1–2 tablespoons

SPICES AND CONDIMENTS
- Dried dill, 2 teaspoons (if not using fresh)
- Hungarian paprika (or regular sweet paprika), 1 tablespoon, or to taste
- Salt, 1 1/2 teaspoons, or to taste
- Pepper, to taste

TOOLS
- Large soup pot
- Blender or food processor
- Decorative soup bowls for serving

Tofu "Sour Cream"

FRUITS
- Lemon, 1 for juicing

WET INGREDIENTS
- Silken tofu, 1 package (12 ounces)

SPICES AND CONDIMENTS
- Salt, to taste

TOOLS
- Blender or food processor

Stuffed Cabbage

For Cabbage Rolls:
VEGETABLES
- Green cabbage, 2 large heads with nice outer leaves (you will need 16 large outer leaves)
- Onion, 1 large
- Garlic, 4 cloves

WET INGREDIENTS
- Vegetable broth, 1/4 cup, or more as needed
- Soy sauce (or gluten-free tamari), 2 tablespoons

DRY INGREDIENTS
- Toasted pine nuts, 3/4 cup
- Dried currants or raisins, 3/4 cup
- Pearled barley, 3/4 cup uncooked (or rice, 1 cup uncooked for gluten-free option)

OPTIONAL
- Tempeh, 3 cups

SPICES AND CONDIMENTS
- Salt, to taste
- Caraway seeds, 1 1/2 teaspoons
- Pepper, to taste

TOOLS
- Large pot
- Tongs or large slotted spoon
- Colander
- Large skillet
- Plate to assemble rolls
- Olive oil cooking spray
- Glass baking dish (9 x 13 inch)
- Parchment paper and aluminum foil
- Optional: Slow cooker

For Cabbage Roll Sauce:
VEGETABLES
- Onion, 1
- Garlic, 2 cloves

WET INGREDIENTS
- Vegetable broth, 1/4 cup, plus more as needed; 2 additional cups
- Tomato paste, two 7-ounce jars
- Strained tomatoes, 2 cups
- Prepared sauerkraut, 3 cups

DRY INGREDIENTS
- Sugar, 2 teaspoons

SPICES AND CONDIMENTS
- Salt, to taste
- Hungarian paprika (or regular sweet paprika), 1 tablespoon
- Pepper, to taste

OPTIONAL
- Tofu "sour cream" (ingredients found with the Mushroom Soup recipe at left)

TOOLS
- Medium saucepan

Pickled Beets

VEGETABLES

Beets, 8 large

Red onions, 2 medium

WET INGREDIENTS

Rice vinegar, 1 cup

White wine vinegar, 1 cup

DRY INGREDIENTS

Sugar, 1/2 cup

SPICES AND CONDIMENTS

Salt, 2 teaspoons

TOOLS

Large pot

Small saucepan

Whisk

Large glass bowl

Ball canning jars (or another canning jar)

Optional: Small decorative bowls

Apple-Cucumber Salad:

VEGETABLES

English cucumbers, 2 large

Red onion, 1 medium

White onion, 1 small

FRUITS

Red apples, 6 medium (2 pounds)

Optional: Lemon, 1 for juicing, only if not using rice vinegar

Wet ingredients:

Silken tofu, 2 cups

Rice vinegar, 1/4 cup

For adult version: Prepared horseradish, 2 tablespoons

DRY INGREDIENTS

Apple chips, 2 cups, for garnish

SPICES AND CONDIMENTS

Salt, 1 teaspoon, or more to taste

TOOLS

Food processor

Large salad bowl

Blender

Tongs

Flodni Parfait

FRUITS

Lemon, 1 large for zesting

Red apples, 3 medium for the apple layer; 2 for garnish

WET INGREDIENTS

Rice milk, 2 cups

Maple syrup, 2 tablespoons; 1/2 cup

All-natural vanilla extract, 4 teaspoons total

Apple juice, 1 cup

Water, 2 cups, if not using jam for the plum/prune jam layer

DRY INGREDIENTS

Brown rice crispy cereal, 4 cups

Ezekial cereal, 2 cups

Chia seeds, 1/3 cup

Poppy seeds, 2 tablespoons

Ground walnuts, 1 1/2 cups

Raisins or dried currants, 1/2 cup

Cornstarch, 2 teaspoons

Prunes (dried plums), 1 1/2 cups, if not using jam for the plum/prune jam layer

OPTIONAL

Sugar, 1 tablespoon in the crunchy layer

Sugar, 2 teaspoons in the apple layer

Alternative liquid sweetener such as honey or agave nectar, if not using maple syrup

Plum jam, if not using prunes for the plum/prune jam layer

SPICES AND CONDIMENTS

Salt, a few pinches

Cinnamon, 1 teaspoon

TOOLS

Medium glass bowl

Microplane zester

Medium airtight container (for the pudding layer)

3 small saucepans

Food processor or potato masher

Parfait glasses, wine glasses, or martini glasses

SIMCHAT TORAH

—

jewishfoodhero.com

Spiced Apple Compote

FRUITS
Red apples, 6 medium
Pears, 2 medium

WET INGREDIENTS
Apple juice, unfiltered and unsweetened, 1 cup, plus more as needed

DRY INGREDIENTS
Optional: Dried currants, 1/2 cup

SPICES AND CONDIMENTS:
Cinnamon, 2 teaspoons
Nutmeg, 1/2 teaspoon
Cloves, 1/2 teaspoon
Cardamom, 1/2 teaspoon

TOOLS
Large saucepan
Small decorative bowls for serving

Biryani Vegetable Rice

VEGETABLES
Onion, 1 medium
Garlic, 2 cloves
Ginger, 1 small chunk
Cauliflower, 1 small head
Carrots, 3 medium
Tomatoes, 2 medium
Green beans, 1 cup

HERBS
Fresh cilantro sprigs, 1 bunch, for garnish

WET INGREDIENTS
Vegetable broth, 1/4 cup, plus more as needed
Water, 5 1/2 cups

DRY INGREDIENTS
Brown basmati rice, 3 cups
Raisins, 1/3 cup
No-salt dry-roasted cashews, 1 cup, for garnish

SPICES AND CONDIMENTS
Bay leaves, 2
Salt, 2 teaspoons
Ground cinnamon, 2 teaspoons
Ground cardamom, 1/2 teaspoon
Ground cloves, 1/2 teaspoon
Curry powder, 1 teaspoon (or more if desired)
Ground coriander, 1/2 teaspoon

TOOLS
Large sauté pan
Large pot
Cooking oil
Deep (4 quart) covered baking dish
Fork
Large serving platter

Warm Cabbage Salad With Peanuts

VEGETABLES
Green cabbage, 1 head
Carrots, 2 medium
Garlic, 2 cloves
Ginger, 1 small chunk
Optional: Fresh green serrano chilies, 1 to 2

HERBS
Fresh cilantro leaves, 1 cup, for garnish

FRUITS
Lemon, 1 for juicing

WET INGREDIENTS
Vegetable broth, 1–2 tablespoons as needed

DRY INGREDIENTS
Finely chopped peanuts, 1/2 cup, for garnish
Dried desiccated unsweetened coconut, shredded or grated, 1/2 cup, for garnish

SPICES AND CONDIMENTS
Salt, 1 teaspoon, or to taste
Turmeric, 1/2 teaspoon
Ground cumin, 1/2 teaspoon
Optional: Toasted mustard seeds, 2 teaspoons

TOOLS
Large glass bowl
Large skillet
Small glass bowl for toasted spices
Large serving bowl

Creamy Lentil Dahl

VEGETABLES
Onions, 4 medium
Ginger, 1 large chunk
Garlic, 9 cloves
Tomatoes, 8 medium, or tomato puree

HERBS
Fresh cilantro sprigs, 1 cup, for garnish

FRUITS
Lemon, 1 for garnish

WET INGREDIENTS
- Water, 9 cups
- Vegetable broth, 1/4 cup, plus more if needed
- Unsweetened rice milk (or other non-dairy milk), 4 1/2 cups

DRY INGREDIENTS
- Red lentils, 3 1/2 cups

SPICES AND CONDIMENTS
- Ground cumin, 1 1/2 tablespoons
- Salt, 1 teaspoon, or to taste

TOOLS
- Large saucepan
- Medium skillet
- Potato masher or immersion blender
- Individual bowls for serving

Pickled Red Onions

VEGETABLES
- Red onions, 2 medium
- Optional: Minced green chilies, 1 tablespoon

FRUITS
- Limes, 2 for juicing

WET INGREDIENTS
- Apple cider vinegar, 1/2 cup

DRY INGREDIENTS
- Sugar, 1 teaspoon

SPICES AND CONDIMENTS
- Salt, 2 teaspoons
- Indian red chili powder, 1 teaspoon

TOOLS
- Medium glass bowl
- Glass jar (clean and preferably boiled to sterilize)
- Several small decorative bowls for serving

Tapioca Pudding

OTHER
- Edible flowers, 8 pieces (such as pansies or rose petals), for garnish

WET INGREDIENTS
- Rice milk or unsweetened almond milk, 3 cups
- Coconut milk, 3 cups (use the unsweetened variety sold in cartons, not canned coconut milk or cream)

DRY INGREDIENTS
- Large tapioca pearls, 1 cup
- Sugar, 1/2 cup
- Ground pistachios, 1/2 cup, for garnish

SPICES AND CONDIMENTS
- Cinnamon or cardamom, sprinkle for garnish

TOOLS
- Medium strainer
- Medium saucepan
- Individual dessert bowls for serving

—

CHANUKAH

—

.jewishfoodhero.com

Banana-Mango Smoothie

FRUITS
Bananas, 4 medium

Mangoes, 2 medium, or one 15-ounce bag of frozen mangoes (look for no sugar added)

WET INGREDIENTS
Non-dairy milk, 4 cups

All-natural vanilla extract, 2 teaspoons

SPICES AND CONDIMENTS
Ground cinnamon, 1 teaspoon

TOOLS
High-powered blender

Small serving cups or shooters

Latkes With Chili Cream and Applesauce

VEGETABLES
White potatoes, 8 medium (4.4 pounds)

Yam, 1 medium

WET INGREDIENTS
Low-fat, non-dairy milk, 1/4 cup

DRY INGREDIENTS
All-purpose flour, or gluten-free all-purpose flour, 1 1/3 cups

Baking powder, 1 teaspoon

SPICES AND CONDIMENTS
Salt, 3 teaspoons

TOOLS
Box grater

Large mixing bowl

2 baking sheets

Parchment paper

Cooking oil spray

Spatula

Large platter for serving

Cinnamon Applesauce

FRUITS
Apples, 12 medium (4.4 pounds)

WET INGREDIENTS
Apple juice, 1 1/2 cups

DRY INGREDIENTS
Raw sugar or maple syrup, 1/4 cup plus 2 tablespoons

SPICES AND CONDIMENTS
Salt, 1 teaspoon

Cinnamon, 1 1/4 teaspoons

TOOLS
Large saucepan

Potato masher (or food processor)

Medium serving bowl

Chili "Sour Cream"

VEGETABLES
Fresh cayenne peppers, 1–2

FRUITS
Lemon, 1 large for juicing

WET INGREDIENTS:
Soft silken tofu, 2 boxes (24 ounces)

DRY INGREDIENTS
Sugar, 3 tablespoons

SPICES AND CONDIMENTS
Salt, 2 teaspoons

Optional: Sweet paprika, for garnish

Optional: Cayenne pepper

TOOLS
Blender or food processor

Medium serving bowl

Bean Salsa Salad With Corn

VEGETABLES
Shallots, 4 medium

Garlic, 8 cloves

Tomatoes, 6

Lettuce, 1 medium head

Cucumbers, 2 medium

Orange bell peppers, 2

HERBS
Cilantro, 1 small bunch, for garnish

FRUITS
Limes, 7 for juicing

WET INGREDIENTS
Kidney beans, two 14-ounce cans

Corn, one 14-ounce can (or 2–3 ears of corn)

Apple cider vinegar, 1 teaspoon

SPICES AND CONDIMENTS
Salt, 3/4 teaspoon

Pepper, 1/2 teaspoon

Cumin, 1/2 teaspoon

CHANUKAH

Shopping list

TOOLS
- *Small bowl*
- *Medium bowl*
- *Large salad bowl*
- *Colander*
- *Optional: Juicer*

Spiced Acorn Squash

VEGETABLES
- *Acorn squash, 4 (7 pounds)*
- *Garlic, 2 cloves*

WET INGREDIENTS
- *Vegetable broth, 2 cups*

SPICES AND CONDIMENTS
- *Chili powder, 1 tablespoon*
- *Ground cumin, 1 tablespoon*
- *Paprika, 1 tablespoon*
- *Oregano, 2 teaspoons*
- *Salt, 1 teaspoon*
- *Cinnamon, 1 teaspoon*

TOOLS
- *2 baking trays*
- *Small bowl*
- *Glass jar with cover, for mixing*
- *Aluminum foil*
- *Large serving platter*

Strawberry-Glazed Sufganiyot

WET INGREDIENTS
- *Coconut milk (can also use almond milk or soy milk), 3/4 cup*
- *Safflower oil, 1/4 cup plus 2 tablespoons*
- *Applesauce, 1/2 cup plus 1 tablespoon*
- *All-natural vanilla extract, 1 1/2 teaspoons*
- *Apple cider vinegar, 3/4 teaspoon*
- *All-fruit strawberry jam, 3/4 cup*

DRY INGREDIENTS
- *Flour, All-purpose or gluten-free flour, 1 1/2 cups*
- *Raw sugar, 3/4 cup*
- *Baking powder, 1 1/4 teaspoons*
- *Baking soda, 1 teaspoon*

SPICES AND CONDIMENTS
- *Salt, 1/2 teaspoon*
- *Cinnamon, 1 teaspoon*

TOOLS
- *Medium mixing bowl*
- *Whisk*
- *Large mixing bowl*
- *1 doughnut pan (this is an absolute requirement)*
- *Cooking oil spray*
- *Small saucepan*
- *Dessert platter*

jewishfoodhero.com

—

TU B'SHVAT

—

Mint Citrus Plate

VEGETABLES
Fennel, 1 large head

HERBS
Fresh mint, 1 small bunch

FRUITS
Lemon, 1 for juicing
Oranges, 5 medium
Grapefruits, 4 medium

WET INGREDIENTS
Balsamic vinegar, 1 1/2 tablespoons

SPICES AND CONDIMENTS:
Salt, 1 teaspoon total

TOOLS
Medium bowl
Serving platter

Gong Bao Garbanzo Beans With Soba Noodles

VEGETABLES
Butternut squash, 1
Kale (or another green leafy vegetable), 2 bunches
Garlic, 2 cloves
Ginger, 3/4-inch segment for mincing
Scallions, 1 bunch (need 6 stems)
Optional: Red chilies, 2 dried

WET INGREDIENTS
Rice vinegar, 3 tablespoons
Vegetable broth, 3/4 cup
Garbanzo beans, 4 cups
Water, 2 tablespoons

DRY INGREDIENTS
Soba noodles or gluten-free spaghetti, 1 pound
Raw sugar or maple syrup, 1/4 cup
Cornstarch or arrowroot, 3 teaspoons

SPICES AND CONDIMENTS
Soy sauce or gluten-free tamari, 1 tablespoon, or to taste
Soy sauce, 1/4 cup
Optional: Sichuan peppercorns, 1 teaspoon

TOOLS
Large pot
Slotted spoon
Colander or strainer
Medium bowl
2 small bowls
Large skillet
Small skillet
Food processor (if using the chilies)
Large serving platter

Tamari-Maple Cabbage Salad

VEGETABLES
Green cabbage (or napa cabbage), 1 medium head
Red cabbage, 1 small head
Carrots, 6 medium
Optional: Scallions, 1 bunch
Ginger, 1-inch chunk
Garlic, 2 medium cloves

FRUITS
Oranges, 2 medium, for juicing

WET INGREDIENTS
Vegetable broth (or water), 1/4 cup
Maple syrup (or unrefined sugar), 3 tablespoons
Rice vinegar, 1/2 cup

SPICES AND CONDIMENTS
Soy sauce or gluten-free tamari, 1/4 cup

TOOLS
Large salad bowl
Small saucepan (2 quart)
Whisk

Green Tea Smoothie With Ginger

VEGETABLES
Ginger, 1/4-inch chunk

FRUITS
Peaches (frozen), 5 cups
Dates, 4–5

WET INGREDIENTS
Green tea, 3 tea bags to make 3 cups of green tea
Vanilla non-dairy yogurt, 2 cups
Pure vanilla extract, 2 teaspoons

TOOLS
Blender
Small serving glasses or shooters

Date Balls (Spicy Version)

FRUITS:
Dates, 16
Optional: Orange, 1 for juicing (may need a few extra drops to moisten the dates)

DRY INGREDIENTS
Almonds, 1/2 cup

SPICES AND CONDIMENTS
Salt, 1/8 tablespoon
Dried red chili pepper, 1 teaspoon,
or to taste
Toasted sesame seeds for the coating

TOOLS
Food processor
Tablespoon
Dessert platter

Date Balls (Sweet Version)

FRUITS
Dates, 16
Optional: Orange, 1 for juicing
(may need a few extra drops to
moisten the dates)

WET INGREDIENTS
Vanilla extract, 1 1/2 teaspoons

DRY INGREDIENTS
Almonds, 1/2 cup
Crushed toasted almonds for the
coating

SPICES AND CONDIMENTS
Salt, 1 pinch

TOOLS
Food processor
Tablespoon
Dessert platter

PURIM

jewishfoodhero.com

PURIM
Shopping list

Pureed Carrot Soup

VEGETABLES
- Fresh butternut squash (if not using canned), 1 medium
- Yellow or white onion, 1 medium
- Carrots, 7 medium

HERBS
- Fresh mint, 1/4 cup, for garnish

WET INGREDIENTS
- Butternut squash puree, one 15-ounce can
- Vegetable broth (or water), 8 cups
- Unsweetened low-fat rice milk (or water), 2 cups

DRY INGREDIENTS
- White rice, 2 tablespoons

SPICES AND CONDIMENTS
- Salt, 1 teaspoon, or to taste
- Freshly ground black pepper, to taste

TOOLS
- Medium pot and steamer basket, if using fresh squash
- Medium bowl, if using fresh squash
- Large soup pot
- Immersion blender
- Individual bowls for serving

Choreschte Lape

VEGETABLES
- Onion, 1 large
- Garlic, 3 cloves
- Baby bella mushrooms, 7 cups

HERBS
- Garnish: fresh mint, 1 bunch

FRUITS
- Lime, 1 large for juicing and zesting

WET INGREDIENTS
- Vegetable broth (or water), 6 cups
- Tomato paste, 1/2 cup
- Fire-roasted diced tomatoes, 1 cup canned (or fresh diced tomatoes, 1 cup)

DRY INGREDIENTS
- Yellow split peas, 2 1/2 cups, or red lentils, 2 cups

SPICES AND CONDIMENTS
- Salt, 1 1/2 teaspoons, or to taste
- Ground cinnamon. 1 teaspoon
- Freshly ground black pepper, to taste

TOOLS
- Large pot
- Large serving bowl

Persian Rice With Currants

HERBS
- Fresh dill, 1 bunch

WET INGREDIENTS
- Water, 8 1/2 cups plus 2 tablespoons total

DRY INGREDIENTS
- White basmati rice, 4 cups
- Dried currants, 1/2 cup

SPICES AND CONDIMENTS
- Salt, 1 1/2 teaspoons, or to taste
- Turmeric, 1/2 teaspoon

TOOLS
- Fine mesh strainer
- Large saucepan
- Cooking oil spray
- Wooden spoon
- 2 paper towels
- Medium bowl
- Small glass bowl
- Large serving platter
- Optional: Electric rice cooker

Cucumber Salad With Creamy Dressing

VEGETABLES
- English cucumbers, 3
- Red onion, 1 small

HERBS
- Fresh mint, 1 bunch
- Fresh parsley, 1 bunch

FRUITS
- Lemon, 1 for juicing

WET INGREDIENTS
- Plain non-dairy yogurt, 1 1/2 cups

DRY INGREDIENTS
- Brown sugar, 2 teaspoons

SPICES AND CONDIMENTS
- Salt, 1 1/2 teaspoons total, or more to taste
- Freshly ground black pepper

TOOLS
- Blender or food processor
- Large glass bowl
- Colander

Hamantaschen Cookies

FRUITS
Orange, 1 for zesting and juicing

WET INGREDIENTS
Unsweetened low-fat non-dairy milk (or water), 3 tablespoons

Virgin coconut oil, 1/2 cup (check the bottle to make sure it can be heated to 350 F)

Vanilla extract, 1 teaspoon

All-fruit jam in the flavor of your choice, 1 jar

DRY INGREDIENTS
Arrowroot flour, 2 tablespoons

All-purpose flour or gluten-free baking mix (such as Bob's Red Mill Gluten Free All Purpose Baking Flour), 2 1/4 cups

Aluminum-free baking powder, 1 teaspoon

Organic cane sugar (evaporated cane juice), 1/2 cup

Optional: Powdered sugar, 1/4 cup, for the cookie garnish

SPICES AND CONDIMENTS
Salt, 1/4 teaspoon

TOOLS
Small bowl

Whisk

Medium mixing bowl

Large mixing bowl

Wooden spoon or electric mixer

Plastic wrap, if chilling the dough

Parchment paper

3-inch round cookie cutter or you can use the rim of a glass

Spatula

Cooking oil

Baking sheet

Cooling rack

Small mesh strainer for sprinkling powdered sugar

—

PESACH

—

jewishfoodhero.com

Parsnip Tahini spread

VEGETABLES
Parsnips, 3 large
Scallions, for 3 teaspoons sliced
Red radishes, for garnish
Beet, 1 small for garnish

HERBS
Parsley, for garnish

WET INGREDIENTS
Tahini, 1/4 cup plus 2 tablespoons
Kosher for Passover white wine vinegar, 1 tablespoon plus 1 teaspoon

SPICES AND CONDIMENTS
Salt, 2 teaspoons
White pepper, to taste

TOOLS
Medium saucepan
Colander
Large bowl
Blender or food processor
Medium serving bowl
Serving plate for matzo

Chilled Pink Cucumber Soup

VEGETABLES
Cucumbers, 3 medium plus 1 for garnish
Scallions, 1 small bunch
Beet, 1 small
Radish, for garnish

HERBS
Fresh dill, 1 small bunch for garnish
Fresh mint, 1 small bunch for garnish

FRUITS
Red apples, 4 medium
Lemons, 3 for juicing

WET INGREDIENTS
Almond milk, 2 cups

DRY INGREDIENTS
Unsalted cashews, 2 cups

SPICES AND CONDIMENTS
Salt, 1 tablespoon, or more to taste
White pepper, to taste

TOOLS
Blender or food processor
Individual soup bowls for serving

Vegetarian Shepherd's Pie

VEGETABLES
Red skinned potatoes, 3 pounds
Onions, 2 medium
Mushrooms, 3 cups
Carrots, 2 large
Cauliflower, 1 small head
Carrots, for the topping
Yellow summer squash, for the topping
Zucchini, for the topping

HERBS
Fresh sage, 1 teaspoon
Fresh thyme, 2 tablespoons

WET INGREDIENTS
Almond milk, 1 cup
Vegetable broth (not low sodium), 3 cups

DRY INGREDIENTS
Potato starch, 3 tablespoons

SPICES AND CONDIMENTS
Pepper, to taste
Salt, 2 teaspoons

TOOLS
Extra large pot
Large skillet
Small bowl
Colander
Potato masher
Glass baking dish (9 x 13 inch)
Large spoon
Medium pot and steamer basket

Green Salad With Fresh Herbs

VEGETABLES
Lettuce, butter crunch and/or green leaf, 4 heads
Scallions, 2 bunches
Shallots, 2 small, or garlic, 4 cloves

HERBS
Fresh mint, 1 bunch
Fresh cilantro, 1 bunch

FRUITS
Limes, 4 small for juicing (for 1/2 cup juice)

WET INGREDIENTS
Liquid sugar cane syrup, 1/2 cup

SPICES AND CONDIMENTS

Salt, 1 teaspoon, or more to taste

TOOLS

Large salad bowl
Salad dressing shaker bottle

Pistachio Apple Cake

FRUITS

Granny Smith apples, 3 large

VEGETABLES

Yellow summer squash, 1 small

WET INGREDIENTS

Applesauce, 1/2 cup
Orange juice, 1/4 cup
Water, 3 tablespoons (for the flax "egg")
Optional: Non-dairy vanilla ice cream, for garnish (if planning to serve hot)

DRY INGREDIENTS

Matzo meal (or matzo cake meal), 3/4 cup
Potato starch, 1/4 cup
Kosher for Passover baking powder, 1 teaspoon
Sugar, 1 1/2 cups total
Ground flax seeds, 1 tablespoon
Unsalted pistachios, 2–3 tablespoons chopped
Optional: Kosher for Passover powdered sugar, for garnish (if planning to serve cool)

SPICES AND CONDIMENTS

Salt, 1/2 teaspoon
Ground cinnamon, 1 teaspoon
Ground nutmeg, 1/4 teaspoon

TOOLS

Medium mixing bowl
Large mixing bowl
Grater
2 small bowls
Cooking oil
8-inch cake pan or springform pan

LAG B'OMER

—

Blueberry Apple Smoothie

VEGETABLES
Cucumbers, 2 small

HERBS
Optional: Fresh mint, 1 small bunch

FRUITS
Blueberries, 2 1/2 cups fresh or frozen

WET INGREDIENTS
Apple juice, 2 1/2 cups
Ice, 2 cups

TOOLS
Blender
Small serving glasses or shooters

Black Bean Bites With Barbecue Sauce

VEGETABLES
Red onion, 1
Sweet potatoes, 4 medium
Scallions, 1 small bunch
Romaine lettuce, 1 head

HERBS
Fresh cilantro, 1 small bunch

WET INGREDIENTS
Vegetable broth (or water), 1/4 cup
Black beans, two 15-ounce cans, or dried beans, 1 1/3 cups

DRY INGREDIENTS
Brown rice, 1/3 cup

Unbleached white flour (or gluten-free all-purpose flour), 1/2 cup

SPICES AND CONDIMENTS
Salt, 1 teaspoon, or to taste
Ketchup, 1/4 cup
Ground cumin, 2 teaspoons

TOOLS
Medium skillet
Colander
Large bowl
Potato masher or fork
Box grater
Parchment paper
Baking sheet
Cooking oil spray
Spatula
Large serving platter

Homemade Barbecue Sauce

WET INGREDIENTS
Ketchup, 1 1/2 cups
Apple cider vinegar, 1 tablespoon
Mustard, 2 tablespoons
Maple syrup, 2 tablespoons
Optional: Vegan Worcestershire sauce, 1 tablespoon

SPICES AND CONDIMENTS
Onion powder, 1 1/2 teaspoons

TOOLS
Small saucepan
Whisk
Medium serving bowl

Green Bean and New Potato Salad

VEGETABLES
New potatoes, 6 cups
Fresh green beans, 4 cups
Red onions or scallions, 1/4 cup, or more to taste

HERBS
Fresh dill, 1 small bunch, or dried dill, 3 teaspoons
Optional: Fresh parsley, 1 small bunch

WET INGREDIENTS
Red wine vinegar, 1/2 cup
Optional: Vegan Worcestershire sauce, 3 teaspoons

DRY INGREDIENTS
Sugar, 2 tablespoons

SPICES AND CONDIMENTS
Salt, 1/2 teaspoon
Grainy mustard, 1/4 cup
Smoked salt or plain sea salt, 3 teaspoons
Freshly ground black pepper, to taste

TOOLS
Large cooking pot with steamer basket
Large bowl
Medium bowl with ice water
Large mesh strainer
Serving bowl
Rubber spatula
Small bowl
Whisk

FRUITS
Peaches, fresh or frozen, 12 medium (3 pounds)
Lemon, 1 for juicing

Nutritious Cornbread

WET INGREDIENTS

Rice milk (unsweetened, low fat) or water, 1 cup

Applesauce, 1/2 cup

Maple syrup, 1/4 cup

DRY INGREDIENTS

Cornmeal, 1 cup

Unbleached white flour or gluten-free all-purpose flour, 1 cup

Baking powder, 2 teaspoons

SPICES AND CONDIMENTS

Salt, 1/2 teaspoon

TOOLS

Large mixing bowl

Whisk

Medium bowl

Cooking oil

8-inch square baking pan

Toothpick

Platter for serving

FRUITS

Peaches, fresh or frozen, 12 medium (3 pounds)

Lemon, 1 for juicing

Maple-Peach Oat Crumble

WET INGREDIENTS

Apple juice, 2 tablespoons

Vanilla extract, 1 1/2 teaspoons

Non-dairy fruit sorbet or non-dairy vanilla ice cream, for garnish

DRY INGREDIENTS

Cornstarch, 1 tablespoon

Brown sugar or maple syrup, 1/4 cup

All-purpose flour or gluten-free all-purpose flour, 1/4 cup plus 2 tablespoons

Quick oats, 3/4 cup

Unbleached flour or gluten-free all-purpose flour, 3/4 cup

Brown sugar, 3/4 cup

SPICES AND CONDIMENTS

Salt, 3/4 teaspoon (in total)

Ground cinnamon, 1/2 teaspoon

TOOLS

Small bowl

Large bowl

Medium bowl

9-inch pie plate

Small individual serving bowls

—

SHAVUOT

—

jewishfoodhero.com

SHAVUOT

Shopping list

Pink Gazpacho

VEGETABLES
- English cucumber, 1
- Optional: Onion, to taste
- Optional: Jalapeño pepper, to taste
- Optional: Red bell pepper, to taste

HERBS
- Fresh mint, 1 small bunch

FRUITS
- Watermelon, one 3-pound melon
- Lemon, 1 for juicing

WET INGREDIENTS
- Apple juice, 1 1/4 cups
- Optional: Honey, to taste

SPICES AND CONDIMENTS
- Salt, 1/2 teaspoon
- Optional: Pepper, to taste

TOOLS
- Blender or food processor
- Shooters or individual small bowls for serving

Creamy Baked Pasta With Bread Crumb Topping

VEGETABLES
- Garlic, 1 large head (8–12 cloves), for roasting
- Shallots, 4–6 medium, for roasting
- Onions, 2
- Button mushrooms, 3 cups

WET INGREDIENTS
- Vegetable broth (or water), 1/2 cup
- Unsweetened, low-fat non-dairy

milk, 4 cups
- Cold water, 1/2 cup

DRY INGREDIENTS
- Uncooked elbow or penne pasta (can use gluten-free), 4 cups
- Nutritional yeast, 6 tablespoons
- Unbleached flour (or cornstarch or arrowroot powder for gluten-free), 1/2 cup
- Breadcrumbs (can use gluten-free), 1/2 cup

SPICES AND CONDIMENTS
- Salt, 1 teaspoon, or to taste
- Onion powder, 1 teaspoon
- Garlic powder, 1/2 teaspoon
- Prepared mustard, 3 teaspoons
- Ground nutmeg, 1/2 teaspoon
- Turmeric powder, 1/2 teaspoon

TOOLS
- Aluminum foil
- Baking sheet
- Medium stockpot
- Colander to drain cooked pasta
- Skillet
- Small bowl
- Large bowl
- Cooking oil
- Glass baking dish (9 x 13 inch)
- Spatula

Joni's 24-Hour Cucumber Salad

VEGETABLES
- English cucumbers, 6 large
- Optional: Red onion, 1 medium

HERBS
- Optional: Fresh dill, 1/4 cup minced

FRUITS
- Orange, 3 for juicing
- Lemon, 2 large for juicing

DRY INGREDIENTS
- Raw sugar or maple syrup, 2 tablespoons

SPICES AND CONDIMENTS
- Salt, 1 1/2 tablespoons
- Grainy mustard, 1/4 cup
- Freshly ground black pepper, to taste

TOOLS
- Food processor with slicing blade
- Large glass bowl
- Small plate
- Colander
- Kitchen towel
- Serving bowl
- Medium bowl
- Whisk

Rainbow Quinoa Salad

VEGETABLES
- Scallions, 2 small bunches
- Carrots, 5 medium
- Red cabbage, 1/4 medium head
- Optional: Garlic, 1 clove

HERBS
- Fresh parsley, 1 large bunch

FRUITS
- Orange, 3 medium for juicing
- Lemon, 2 medium for juicing

SHAVUOT

Shopping list

WET INGREDIENTS
Low-sodium vegetable broth or water, 4 cups

DRY INGREDIENTS
Raw quinoa, 1 cup plus 3 tablespoons

SPICES AND CONDIMENTS
Salt, 1 1/2 teaspoons, or to taste

Pepper, to taste

TOOLS
Mesh strainer

Medium saucepan

Fork

Large mixing bowl

Small bowl

Whisk

Lemon "Cheesecake"

FRUITS
Lemon, 4 for juicing and for garnish

Fresh berries of your choice, for garnish

WET INGREDIENTS
Silken tofu, 2 boxes (24 ounces)

Vanilla, 2 teaspoons

Tahini, 2 tablespoons

DRY INGREDIENTS
Graham crackers, 1 box (about 30 crackers)

Dried dates, about 3 large

Sugar, 2 cups

SPICES AND CONDIMENTS
Salt, 1 1/4 teaspoons total

TOOLS
Food processor

Cooking oil

Springform cheesecake pan (8 inch)

Offset spatula

Dessert platter for serving

INDEX

jewishfoodhero.com

jewishfoodhero.com

N

O

V

W

Y

Z

JEWISH FOOD HERO

Nourishing your mind, body, and spirit

ABOUT AND GRATITUDE

ABOUT KENDEN ALFOND AND JEWISH FOOD HERO

Kenden Alfond is the founder of Jewish Food Hero, which nourishes the minds, bodies, and spirits of Jewish women around the globe. She offers vegan recipes that are a modern twist on traditional Jewish meals to support an intuitive turning toward greater health, as well as inspiring resources to support women as they engage in Jewish life and foster self-connection. Grab her free guide, 18 Effortless Ways to Eat Less Meat and Dairy, at JewishFoodHero.com.

GRATITUDE

I deeply appreciate all the people who contributed to this cookbook. I couldn't have done it without them.

Photography:
Matkonation

Design Studio:
One Plus One Design

Editor:
The Studio of Ana Ottman

Recipe Advisors and Testers:
Each and every person who has eaten at my house for Shabbat, Christine Waltermyer, Giulia Cucci, Sam Wise, Jessica Halfin, Charles Vincent (my husband), and Yaël Alfond-Vincent (my daughter).

Questions? Reach out to *hello@jewishfoodhero.com.*